The
Cocktail Year

The Cocktail Year

'Charles'

Contributing Editor
Sue Parkin

Arco Publishing, Inc.
New York

Acknowledgments

Photographs Mike O'Neill
Props for photographs The Cocktail Shop,
30 Neal St, Covent Garden, London WC2
and Le Pot, King Edward Court, Windsor

Published 1985 by Arco Publishing, Inc.
215 Park Avenue South, New York, NY 10003

Hardback ISBN 0–668–06396–3
Paperback ISBN 0–668–06400–5

Printed in Hong Kong

CONTENTS

The drinks are introduced on the dates below.

INTRODUCTION

The Cocktail Year contains 365 cocktails, one for every day of the year. There are mouthwatering cocktails for all occasions: romantic cocktails to lure your lover on Valentine's day, cool blue cocktails to sip by the pool on long summer days and warming punches for winter parties. Each cocktail is illustrated in full colour to give you an idea of what it looks like, what glass to serve it in and how to garnish it.

You can use *The Cocktail Year* as a cocktail-maker's diary. Space has been left for you to write in your own comments on your cocktail-making extravaganzas, your friends' birthdays, and to remind yourself of other occasions worth celebrating with a seasonal cocktail. Mark your own special occasions by making the cocktail for that day.

The book assumes that your drinks cupboard is empty at the start of the year. You can then start adding drinks, one by one (46 drinks are added at approximately weekly intervals) and at each stage have a large selection of cocktails to choose from. Gradually a good stock of drinks will be accumulated and the more complex cocktail ideas are then suggested. Any cocktail given on a specific date will only contain the drinks that have been introduced by that date.

Preparing cocktails is simplified if ingredients, basic equipment and glasses are stored together. The location will obviously depend on space available: kitchen cupboards, a cocktail cabinet or shelves in a living room. Since it's fun to prepare cocktails in the presence of your guests a trolley may be thought of as an excellent choice and would be a real conversation piece at the start of any occasion.

How to find the cocktail you want to make

1. If you know the name of the cocktail, there is an alphabetical list on page 118.
2. If you want a cocktail for a particular occasion, look it up under the date.
3. If you want a particular kind of cocktail e.g. a party cocktail, a non-alcoholic cocktail, an after-dinner cocktail or a nourishing night-cap look at the lists on page 117 where you will find suggestions.
4. If you want a cheaper cocktail with fewer ingredients, look at the cocktails at the beginning of the book.
5. If you only have a couple of bottles in your drinks cabinet look at the *Ingredients Guide* on page 114 which will tell you which cocktails you can make with them.

Follow this book and you're going to have a great year!

The basic equipment needed is as follows:

1. A shaker. This looks something like a miniature Thermos flask, and consists simply of two nickel containers that fit into each other.
2. A mixing glass. This is simply a large tumbler or bar glass.
3. A mixing spoon. This is a spoon holding about the same amount as a teaspoon, but with a long, thin handle.
4. A strainer.
5. A lemon squeezer.
6. A muddler. This is an implement used for crushing sugar or bruising fruit, mint, etc.
7. A gill measure graded with various fractional parts.

The above are the essentials. Of the other forms of equipment many are part of the normal culinary equipment. Obviously a corkscrew and bottle opener are required, and for certain recipes a nutmeg grater will be needed. A fruit knife and a fork and spoon for handling fruit will be wanted, too, and there should be an ice pick and a scoop or tongs for handling ice. Finally, straws are needed for the longer drinks, and a bundle of cherry sticks to allow simple manipulation of the cherries, olives, etc., that are served in certain cocktails.

Decanter bottles with stoppers are desirable for ingredients that have to be served in the small measurements known as dashes.

A few cocktails are best made in an electric blender.

Glasses

The photographs and recipes will give you a good guide as to the ideal glass to use, but here is a list of the glasses available for serving drinks. Measurements are reckoned in fractions of a gill, which is ¼ of a pint:

1. Cocktail glasses. Each holds about ½ gill.
2. Small wine-glasses or crusta glasses. Each holds about ¾ gill.
3. Wine-glasses. Each holds about 1 gill.
4. Tumblers or highball glasses. Each holds about ½ pint, or 2 gills.
5. Sherbet glasses are like small tumblers.
6. Liqueur glasses. Each holds about ¼ gill. However, fine liqueurs are generally served in large 'balloon' glasses. For ordinary purposes a half-filled cocktail glass is suitable for the serving of a liqueur.
7. Pousse café glasses. Also known as *petites flutes*. Each holds about ⅜ gill.
8. Hot drinks glasses vary in size but have handles.

If you are using a fluid oz, rather than a gill measure remember 1 gill = 5 fluid oz.

Mixers and garnishes

Although you are building up a drinks cabinet with drinks that will keep, you will need to buy mixers as you need them. Once opened they will not keep so are not included in the overall plan for accumulating drinks.

The following are used as mixers in this book: ginger ale, milk, soda water, ale, wine, sparkling wine, cider and champagne.

Often it is the garnish that makes the cocktail look spectacular. The photographs and recipes will give you ideas for garnishing your cocktails, but look round the cocktail shops or departments of the big stores for other ideas.

Non-Alcoholic Extras

The spirits and liqueurs will be accumulated over a number of months, but there are a few extra ingredients which will be required. Many of which may already be in your store cupboard.

The following ingredients are used on one occasion at least, during the year. The fresh ingredients should be purchased as you need them. The bitters and syrups will keep almost indefinitely, so buy and store them with your spirits.

1. Bitters: Angostura, orange, secrestat, peach.
2. Fruit: lime, lemon, orange, pineapple, cherries (fresh and maraschino), tangerine, apple.
3. Syrups and juices: orange juice, lime cordial, grape juice, pineapple juice, lemon squash, gooseberry syrup, sirop de citron, vanilla syrup, ginger syrup, cherry syrup, orgeat syrup, fraisette (strawberry syrup), maple syrup, grenadine syrup, grapefruit juice.
4. Sugar in lump, powder or syrup form.
5. Eggs.
6. Fresh double cream (sometimes sweetened with a little sugar syrup).
7. Coconut cream.
8. Miscellaneous: Blackcurrant jelly, anisette, Worcester sauce, tomato ketchup, lemon water ice, rock candy, pickled onion, olive.

It is worth having the following most common extras to hand when mixing cocktails: Angostura and orange bitters, grenadine syrup, sugar syrup.

EIGHT SIMPLE RULES TO COCKTAIL MAKING

1. Do follow the recipe, measure the ingredients and work methodically so that you're in no doubt as to the ingredients you have or have not yet added to the shaker or mixing glass. Unless otherwise stated, each cocktail recipe provides a single drink.

2. Use bitters and syrups with care, a slight error may spoil the drink.

3. A *dash* is equivalent to ¹/₃ of a teaspoon. Approximately 50 dashes to the gill.

4. **Shaken cocktails**. Place some ice in the shaker, either cracked or cubes and add the ingredients. Replace the upper part of the shaker and holding it with both hands (one being held over the upper part to prevent accidents and spillage) shake briskly to mix and cool ingredients. Too much shaking will melt the ice and dilute the drink. Strain into the glass. *Do not shake* sparkling drinks e.g. champagne, soda water etc.

5. **Stirred or Mixed Cocktails**. The ingredients are placed in a mixing glass with ice then stirred with a mixing spoon, briskly (unless otherwise stated) until the ingredients are mixed and cooled. Strain into the glass.

6. **Blended Cocktails**. Blend the ingredients with the specified amount of crushed ice for a few seconds (not longer or the cocktail will be too diluted). Pour into the glass.

7. **Ice**. Always keep a good supply in the freezer or ice compartment in the refrigerator. There are ice making appliances on the market, which must be the ideal for the serious cocktail maker.

8. Lemon peel is often required to be squeezed on top of the drink. For this, a thin piece of peel should be taken between the fingers and gently squeezed or twisted, so that the juice drops into the drink. The lemon peel should never be put in the glass unless the recipe says so.

JANUARY

GIN

1ˢᵗ Bulldog Cooler

1 or 2 dashes of sugar syrup
The juice of half an orange
½ gill of dry gin
⅓ pint of ginger ale

Place a lump of ice in a tumbler, add ingredients, stir well. Serve with a slice of orange.

New Year's Day

2ⁿᵈ Pink Lady Cocktail

The white of an egg
1 tablespoonful of grenadine
½ gill of dry gin

Use the shaker. Serve with a cherry.

3ʳᵈ Orange Blossom Cocktail (1)

¼ gill of fresh orange juice
¼ gill of dry gin

Use the shaker.

'Choose thy company before thy drink,' – an old English proverb. There's a drink to suit everyone's taste in this book.

4ᵗʰ Gimlet Cocktail

⅓ gill of dry gin
⅙ gill of lime cordial

Use the mixing glass. Serve with a slice of lime or kiwi fruit.

5ᵗʰ Cream Fizz

1 teaspoonful of sugar syrup
The juice of one lemon
1 teaspoonful of fresh double cream
¾ gill of dry gin

Use a shaker, strain into a highball glass, add ice. Top up with soda water, if desired, stir. Serve with straws.

Always have a good supply of lemons, they are used in many cocktails.

6ᵗʰ Hot Gin

The juice of one lemon
2 lumps of sugar
½ gill of dry gin

Put ingredients in a glass, fill up with boiling water, stir well, and serve with a slice of lemon.

This one will keep the cold out!

7ᵗʰ Grape Vine Cocktail

1 dash of grenadine
⅛ gill of fresh lemon juice
⅛ gill of fresh grape juice
¼ gill of dry gin

Use the shaker

 From left: Hot Gin, Gimlet, Bulldog Cooler, Pink Lady Cocktail, Orange Blossom Cocktail (1), Grape Vine Cocktail, Cream Fizz.

JANUARY

ITALIAN VERMOUTH

8th Martini Cocktail (sweet)

⅙ gill of Italian vermouth
⅓ gill of dry gin

Use the mixing glass. Serve with a little lemon-peel juice squeezed on top.

Italian is the sweet vermouth. As it is basically a wine it will deteriorate once opened and should be drunk within a month, which shouldn't be difficult.

9th Club Cooler

1 dash of lemon juice
⅙ gill of grenadine
⅓ gill of Italian vermouth
½ pint of soda water

Place a lump of ice in a tumbler. Add the ingredients, stir well.

Squeeze a little lemon juice on top, and serve with straws.

10th Raymond Hitch Cocktail

The juice of half an orange
1 dash of orange bitters
1 slice of pineapple, to serve
½ gill of Italian vermouth

Use the shaker.

11th Pink Rose Cocktail

1 teaspoonful of grenadine
1 teaspoonful of fresh lemon juice
1 teaspoonful of double cream
* sweetened with a little sugar*
* syrup*

The white of one egg
½ gill of dry gin

Use the shaker. Serve with a cherry.

12th Bennett Cocktail

2 dashes of Angostura bitters
⅓ gill of dry gin
⅙ gill of lime juice

Use the shaker. Serve with a slice of lime.

13th Clover Club Cocktail

The white of an egg
The juice of a fresh lime (or half
* a lemon)*
⅙ gill of grenadine
⅓ gill of dry gin

Use the shaker.

14th Velocity Cocktail

⅓ gill of Italian vermouth
⅙ gill of dry gin

Use the shaker. Serve with a slice of orange.

From left: Martini Cocktail (sweet), Clover Club Cocktail, Bennett Cocktail, Velocity Cocktail, Raymond Hitch Cocktail, Pink Rose Cocktail, Club Cooler.

DUBONNET

15th Dubonnet Cocktail

¼ gill of Dubonnet
¼ gill of dry gin

Use the mixing glass. Serve with a little lemon-peel juice squeezed on top.

Dubonnet is a French aromatic wine.

16th Café Royal Appetiser Cocktail

The juice of half an orange
¼ gill of Dubonnet
¼ gill of dry gin

Use the shaker. Serve with a slice of orange.

17th Gin Sling

¾ gill of dry gin
Sugar syrup according to taste.

Put the ingredients in a tumbler containing a lump of ice. Fill up with water or soda water as desired.

18th Alfonso Cocktail

1 lump of sugar
2 dashes of Secrestat bitter
½ gill of Dubonnet
½ gill of champagne

Put the lump of sugar in a wine-glass, and add the Secrestat bitter. Then add one lump of ice and the

Dubonnet and stir gently. Fill up with champagne, and serve with a little lemon-peel juice squeezed on top.

19th Angostura Fizz

⅛ gill of sugar syrup
¼ gill of Angostura bitters
½ gill of lemon juice
The white of an egg

Use a shaker, strain into a highball glass, add ice. Top up with soda water, if

desired. Stir. Serve with straws.

Angostura is named after the town in Venezuela, where the aromatic bitters were first made in 1824. The same recipe is still used, though Angostura bitters are now produced in Trinidad.

20th Royal Cocktail

1 dash of Angostura bitters
1 dash of orange bitters
⅙ gill of Dubonnet
⅓ gill of dry gin

Use the mixing glass. Serve with a cherry and a little lemon-peel juice squeezed on top.

21st Cider Cocktail

1 dash of Angostura bitters
¾ gill of cider
½ teaspoonful of sugar syrup

Use the mixing glass, half filled with broken ice. Stir well. Strain into a glass. Serve with a slice of lemon

on top. Non-alcoholic cider may be used.

Clockwise from left: Cider Cocktail, Alfonso Cocktail, Dubonnet Cocktail, Angostura Fizz, Gin Sling, Café Royal Appetiser Cocktail, Royal Cocktail (centre).

JANUARY

FRENCH VERMOUTH

		Your Own Special Occasions and Cocktail Rating.
22ⁿᵈ Martini Cocktail (dry) *1 dash of orange bitters* *⅙ gill of Martini vermouth (dry)* *⅓ gill of dry gin*	Use the mixing glass. Serve with a little lemon-peel juice squeezed on top and a slice of lemon.	An all-time classic.
23ʳᵈ Queen's Cocktail *1 slice of crushed pineapple* *⅛ gill of French vermouth* *⅛ gill of Italian vermouth* *¼ gill of dry gin*	Use the mixing glass. Decorate with a small piece of pineapple.	
24ᵗʰ R.A.C. Cocktail *1 dash of orange bitters* *1 dash of grenadine* *⅛ gill of French vermouth* *⅛ gill of Italian vermouth* *¼ gill of dry gin*	Use the mixing glass. Serve with a cherry and a little orange-peel juice squeezed on top.	
25ᵗʰ Yellow Rattler Cocktail *⅛ gill of fresh orange juice* *⅛ gill of French vermouth* *⅛ gill of Italian vermouth* *⅛ gill of dry gin*	Use the shaker. Serve with a small crushed pickled onion.	
26ᵗʰ Polo Cocktail *The juice of half a lime or quarter of a lemon* *⅓ gill of French vermouth* *⅓ gill of Italian vermouth* *⅓ gill of dry gin*	Use the shaker. Serve with a slice of lemon.	*French* as it has always been called, is the dry aromatized wine. It deteriorates once opened, it is suggested that it should be drunk within two weeks of opening.
27ᵗʰ Orange Blossom Cocktail (2) *1 dash of orange bitters* *1 dash of grenadine* *¼ gill of orange juice* *¼ gill of dry gin*	Use the shaker. Serve with a small slice of orange.	
28ᵗʰ Royal Fizz *1 teaspoonful of sugar syrup or grenadine* *The juice of one lemon* *1 egg* *¾ gill of dry gin*	Use a shaker. Strain into a highball glass, add ice. Top up with soda water. Serve with straws.	A fizz is always shaken, which gives the drink a good consistency.

16

 From left: Martini Cocktail (dry), Queen's Cocktail, R.A.C. Cocktail, Royal Fizz, Yellow Rattler Cocktail, Polo Cocktail, Orange Blossom Cocktail (2).

SCOTCH WHISKY

	Your Own Special Occasions and Cocktail Ratings

29th Thistle Cocktail

2 dashes of Angostura bitters
¼ gill of Italian vermouth
¼ gill of Scotch whisky

Use the mixing glass.

30th Scotch Mist Cocktail

⅓ gill of Scotch whisky
cracked ice
twist of lemon peel

Use old-fashioned glasses. Shake Scotch whisky with cracked ice and pour unstrained. Add twist of lemon peel. Serve with straws.

31st Whisky Toddy

1 teaspoonful of sugar
¾ gill of Scotch whisky

Dissolve the sugar in hot water, and add the whisky. Fill up with boiling water. Serve with a slice of lemon on top.

Spending a day outside or in the country? Make up a flask of this toddy to keep you warm.

1st Gaelic Coffee

Hot coffee
2 teaspoonfuls of sugar
⅓ gill of Scotch whisky
fresh double cream

Pour coffee into a glass, stir in sugar and whisky. Pour the cream very gently over the back of a warmed spoon, *Do not stir.*

2nd Affinity Cocktail

2 dashes of Angostura bitters
⅙ gill of French vermouth
⅙ gill of Italian vermouth
⅙ gill of Scotch whisky

Use the mixing glass. Serve with a cherry and a little lemon-peel juice squeezed on top.

3rd Wembley Cocktail

⅙ gill of fresh pineapple juice
⅙ gill of French vermouth
⅙ gill of Scotch whisky

Use the shaker.

4th Whisky Cooler

2 dashes of orange bitters
½ gill of Scotch whisky
½ pint of soda water

Place a lump of ice in a tumbler, add ingredients, stir well, and serve with a slice of orange. If you want to make it sweeter, include one or two dashes of sugar syrup.

 Clockwise from left: Affinity Cocktail, Thistle Cocktail, Scotch Mist Cocktail, Wembley Cocktail, Whisky Cooler, Gaelic Coffee, Whisky Toddy.

FEBRUARY

PERNOD

5th Appetiser Cocktail

1 dash of pernod
¼ gill of Dubonnet
¼ gill of dry gin

Use the shaker. Serve with a little lemon-peel juice squeezed on top.

Pernod is a popular aniseed flavoured aperitif. In France the French drink it well-chilled, mixed with water. It is also a good addition to many cocktails.

6th Duchess Cocktail

⅙ gill of French (or dry Martini) vermouth
⅙ gill of Italian vermouth
⅙ gill of pernod

Use the mixing glass.

7th Whiz-bang Cocktail

2 dashes of pernod
2 dashes of grenadine
2 dashes of orange bitters
⅙ gill of French vermouth
⅓ gill of Scotch whisky

Use the mixing glass. Serve with a slice of orange.

8th Nick's Own Cocktail

1 dash of Angostura bitters
1 dash of pernod
¼ gill of Italian vermouth

Use the mixing glass. Serve with a cherry and a little lemon-peel juice squeezed on top.

9th Belmont Cocktail

1 teaspoonful of sweet cream
⅙ gill of grenadine
⅓ gill of dry gin

Use the shaker.

10th Tiger's Tail Cocktail

⅓ gill of pernod
⅔ gill of orange juice
slice of orange

Serve over ice. Use old-fashioned glass (a small tumbler).

11th White Horse Daisy

2 dashes of grenadine
½ gill of lemon juice
1 teaspoonful of pernod
The white of an egg
½ gill of White Horse whisky

Shake well, and strain. The flavour may be improved if a dash of anisette is added. Serve in an ice-filled tumbler. Top up with soda water. Stir and decorate with fruit.
Alternative serving: strain into ice-filled wine glass, omit soda. Decorate with fruit. Half quantities for this method.

From left: Nick's Own Cocktail, White Horse Daisy, Duchess Cocktail, Whiz-bang Cocktail, Belmont Cocktail, Appetiser Cocktail, Tiger's Tail Cocktail.

BRANDY

12th Presto Cocktail

For four persons:
4 dashes of pernod
⅓ gill of fresh orange juice
⅓ gill of Italian vermouth
1⅓ gills of brandy

Use the mixing glass. Serve with a slice of orange.

13th Plain Egg Nog

1 egg
1 teaspoonful of sugar syrup
¾ gill of brandy or rum
¾ gill of milk

Prepare in a shaker, half-filled with broken ice. Strain into a glass. Sprinkle with grated nutmeg. Stir in more milk if desired.

* If a creamier consistency is preferred use cream instead of milk, or a mixture of milk and cream.

14th Valentine's Champagne Cocktail

1 lump of sugar
2 dashes of Angostura bitters
2 pieces of lemon peel
Champagne

One bottle of champagne will make six cocktails. Put a lump of sugar in a glass, and add the Angostura bitters. Then squeeze the juice of one piece of lemon-peel into the glass. Add an ice cube, and fill with champagne. Stir gently, then squeeze the juice of the other piece of lemon-peel on top.

St. Valentine's Day

15th Washington Cocktail

2 dashes of Angostura bitters
2 dashes of sugar syrup
⅙ gill of brandy
⅓ gill of French vermouth

Use the mixing glass.

16th Linstead Cocktail

1 dash of pernod
¼ gill of sweetened pineapple
*   juice*
¼ gill of Scotch whisky

Use the shaker. Serve with a little lemon-peel juice squeezed on top.

17th Cider Cup (1)

1 gill of brandy
The juice of one lemon
1 quart of cider, preferably
*   chilled*
1 bottle of soda water, preferably
*   chilled*

Place a large piece of ice in a glass jug or bowl, add ingredients and stir.

Decorate with slices of orange and apple. Serve immediately (Serves 4).

18th Charles Cocktail

1 dash of Angostura bitters
¼ gill of Italian vermouth
¼ gill of brandy

Use the mixing glass.

 Clockwise from left: Plain Egg Nog, Cider Cup (1), Valentine's Champagne Cocktail, Linstead Cocktail, Washington Cocktail, Presto Cocktail, Charles Cocktail.

COINTREAU

19th Claret Cup

¼ gill of Cointreau
½ gill of brandy
1 teaspoonful of lemon juice
1 bottle of claret, preferably chilled

1 bottle of soda water, preferably chilled.

Place a large piece of ice in a glass jug or bowl, add ingredients and stir well. Decorate with fruit. Serve immediately. Serves 4.

Cointreau is very refined, colourless, orange-flavoured liqueur. It is made in the Anjou district of France.

20th Hula-hula Cocktail

1 or 2 dashes of Cointreau
⅙ gill of fresh orange juice
⅙ gill of dry gin

Use the shaker.

21st Luigi Cocktail

1 teaspoonful of grenadine
1 dash of Cointreau
The juice of half a tangerine
¼ gill of French vermouth
¼ gill of dry gin

Use the shaker. Serve with a little lemon-peel juice squeezed and served on top.

22nd Egg Sour

1 egg
¼ gill of Cointreau
¼ gill of brandy
3 dashes of lemon juice
Sugar or sugar syrup to taste

Prepare in the shaker, half-filled with broken ice. Shake well, and strain into a glass.

23rd Wyoming Swing Cocktail

The juice of a quarter of an orange
½ teaspoonful of castor sugar
¼ gill of French vermouth
¼ gill of Italian vermouth

Use the mixing glass. Serve in a wine glass and top with soda water.

24th Rolls-Royce Cocktail

⅙ gill of brandy
⅙ gill of Cointreau
⅙ gill of orange juice
egg white

Use the shaker.

25th Monkey Gland Cocktail

2 dashes of pernod
2 dashes of grenadine
⅙ gill of fresh orange juice
⅓ gill of dry gin

Use the shaker. Serve with a kumquat (available at this time of year) or a cocktail cherry.

Kumquats are mainly imported, from Morocco and are eaten with the skin. If they are plentiful, freeze some for later in the year.

From left: Monkey Gland Cocktail, Egg Sour, Hula-hula Cocktail, Luigi Cocktail, Claret Cup, Wyoming Swing Cocktail, Rolls Royce Cocktail.

CRÈME DE MENTHE

26th Alexander's Sister Cocktail

⅛ gill of crème de menthe
⅛ gill of sweet cream
¼ gill of dry gin

Use the shaker.

Crème de menthe is a grain spirit, flavoured with peppermint and sweetened. It is sold in its natural colourless state or coloured green.

27th Oranges and Lemons Cocktail

1 orange
1 lemon
2 or 3 cherries
1 dash of crème de menthe
2 teaspoonfuls of powdered sugar

Peel the orange and lemon, separate into sections, and place in a sundae glass. Put the cherries in the middle, and add the crème de menthe. Serve with powdered sugar on top. To frost the glass: moisten edges of glass with crème de menthe then dip in castor sugar.

28th Brandy Sour

1 teaspoonful of sugar syrup
The juice of half a lemon (or
* equal parts of lemon and lime)*
½ gill of brandy

Mix in a shaker, half-filled with broken ice. Strain into a small wine glass or a brandy glass. If desired add a little soda water and decorate with fruit (e.g. lemon or lime slices).

29th Glad Eye Cocktail

⅙ gill of crème de menthe
⅓ gill of pernod

Use the shaker.

Leap Year Day. If there's a 29th this year, make it an occasion to try this drink – it's delicious.

1st Third Degree Cocktail

4 dashes of pernod
⅙ gill of French vermouth
⅓ gill of dry gin

Use the mixing glass. Serve with an olive.

St. David's Day – patron saint of Wales.

2nd Journalist Cocktail

2 dashes of fresh lemon juice
2 dashes of Cointreau
1 dash of Angostura bitters
1/12 gill of French vermouth
1/12 gill of Italian vermouth
⅓ gill of dry gin

Use the shaker. Serve with a slice of orange and lemon.

3rd Morning Glory Fizz

½ teaspoonful of sugar syrup
The juice of half a lemon
The white of an egg
2 dashes of pernod
¾ gill of Scotch whisky

Use a shaker, strain into a highball glass, add ice. Top up with soda water, if desired. Stir. Serve with straws.

Don't let the name put you off making it any time of the day or night!

 From left: Morning Glory Fizz, Glad Eye Cocktail, Brandy Sour, Oranges and Lemons Cocktail, Third Degree Cocktail, Journalist Cocktail, Alexander's Sister Cocktail.

DRY SHERRY

4th Roc-a-coe Cocktail

¼ *gill of sherry*
¼ *gill of dry gin*

Use the mixing glass. Serve with a cherry.

5th Brazil Cocktail

1 dash of Angostura bitters
1 dash of pernod
¼ *gill of French vermouth*
¼ *gill of dry sherry*

Use the mixing glass. Serve with a little lemon-peel juice squeezed on top.

6th Addington Cocktail

¼ *gill of French vermouth*
¼ *gill of Italian vermouth*

Use the mixing glass. Serve in a wine-glass, top with soda, squeeze a little orange-peel juice and serve on top.

A perfect aperitif.

7th Ale Posset

1 pint of milk
1 cupful (8 fl oz) of sherry
1 cupful (8 fl oz) of ale
4 lumps of sugar

Heat the milk until it almost boils. Meanwhile mix the sherry, ale, and sugar in a jug, and to this add the hot milk. Serve with grated nutmeg. (Serves 3.)

8th Rob Roy Cocktail

⅙ *gill of Scotch whisky*
⅙ *gill of sweet vermouth*
1 dash of Angostura bitters

Use the mixing glass. Add cherry.

9th Whiz-bang Cooler

½ *gill of dry gin*
½ *pint of ginger ale*

Place a lump of ice in a tumbler, add ingredients, stir well, and serve with a dash of crème de menthe and a sprig of mint on top.

10th Grapefruit and Orangeade

2 grapefruits
1 gill of orange juice
1 gill of cider (or apple juice)
¼ *lb of loaf sugar*
Soda water

Rub the loaf sugar on the rind of the grapefruits and oranges, put into a jug. Pour over strained grapefruit and orange juice. Stir to dissolve sugar. Just prior to serving add cider, soda water and ice. Decorate with slices of oranges, apples and grapefruit if you like.

 Clockwise from left: Ale Posset, Roc-a-coe Cocktail, Addington Cocktail, Brazil Cocktail, Grapefruit and Orangeade, Whiz-bang Cooler, Rob Roy Cocktail.

GREEN CHARTREUSE

11th St. Germain Cocktail

The juice of half a lemon
The juice of a quarter of a
grapefruit
The white of one egg
½ gill of green Chartreuse

Use the shaker.

An ancient herbal
liqueur from France.
Green or yellow
varieties are available,
the green is stronger
and the yellow is
sweeter.

12th Orange Fizz

1 teaspoonful of sugar syrup
The juice of one orange
¾ gill dry gin

Use a shaker, strain into a
highball glass, add ice. Top
up with soda water, stir.

Serve with straws and a slice
of orange.

13th Moselle Cobbler

3 or 4 dashes of sugar syrup
1 or 2 dashes of lemon juice
4 dashes of brandy
1 gill Moselle

Make in a shaker, half-filled
with broken ice. Strain into
a tumbler half-full of broken
ice. Serve with a straw.

14th Champs Elysées Cocktail

1 dash of Angostura bitters
⅛ gill of Chartreuse
⅛ gill of sweetened lemon juice
¼ gill of brandy

Use the shaker.

15th Brandy Daisy

¼ gill of grenadine
½ gill of lemon juice
½ gill of lime juice
½ gill of brandy

Shake well, and strain into
an ice-filled tumbler. Top up
with soda water. Stir and
decorate with fruit.
Alternative serving: Strain

into an ice-filled wine glass,
omit soda water. Decorate
with fruit. Half quantities for
this method.

16th Pussy Foot Cocktail

⅓ gill of fresh orange juice
⅓ gill of fresh lemon juice
⅓ gill of lime juice
1 dash of grenadine
yolk of an egg

Use the shaker.

17th Emerald Cooler

Juice of half a lemon
½ gill of brandy
¼ gill of green crème de menthe
1 gill of pineapple juice

Stir ingredients in a tumbler,
add ice. Serve with straws.

St Patrick's Day
(Ireland's Patron Saint).

 Clockwise from top left: Champs Elysées Cocktail, Orange Fizz, Brandy Daisy, Moselle Cobbler, St. Germain Cocktail, Pussy Foot Cocktail, Emerald Cooler.

MARCH

CANADIAN CLUB WHISKY

18th New York Cooler

¼ gill of lemon squash
3 dashes of grenadine
½ gill of Canadian Club whisky
⅓ pint of soda water.

Place a lump of ice in a tumbler, add ingredients. Stir well. Squeeze a little

lemon peel juice on top and serve with a slice of lemon.

Canadian whisky was originally made by Scots and Irish settlers in Canada. It is a light-bodied whisky well suited to cocktails and mixing.

19th Rock and Rye Cocktail

1 piece of rock candy
The juice of one lemon
½ gill of Canadian Club whisky

Dissolve the rock candy in the whisky, and add the lemon juice.

20th Soul's Kiss Cocktail

For four persons:
⅓ gill of fresh orange juice
⅓ gill of Dubonnet
⅔ gill of French vermouth
⅔ gill of Canadian Club whisky

Use the shaker. Serve with slices of orange.

21st Mountain Cocktail

The white of one egg
1/12 gill of fresh lemon juice
1/12 gill of French vermouth
1/12 gill of Italian vermouth
¼ gill of Canadian Club whisky

Use the shaker.

Also good drunk at lower altitudes!

22nd Los Angeles Cocktail

For four persons:
1 dash of Italian vermouth
The juice of one lemon

1 egg
4 teaspoonfuls of sugar
2 gills of Canadian Club whisky

Use the shaker.

23rd Black Velvet Cocktail

Half cold Guinness
Half chilled dry champagne

Serve in ½ pint or 1 pint measures; add Guinness to champagne.

24th Café de Paris Cocktail

3 dashes of anisette, or pernod
   with a dash of sugar syrup
The white of one egg
1 teaspoonful of fresh cream
½ gill of dry gin

Use the shaker.

 Clockwise from left: Soul's Kiss Cocktail, Rock and Rye Cocktail, Café de Paris Cocktail, Black Velvet Cocktail, New York Cooler, Los Angeles Cocktail, Mountain Cocktail.

March

WHITE RUM

25th Cuba Libre Cocktail

The juice of half a lime
Peel of half a lime in one piece
⅓ gill of white rum
Coca-Cola

Place juice and peel of the lime in a tumbler, add ice, rum and fill up with Coca-Cola. Stir and serve.

26th Spring Shake-Up

3 dashes of grenadine
1 dash of Angostura bitters
⅛ gill of Cointreau
¼ gill of white rum
¾ gill of pineapple juice

Shake all ingredients together, strain into a tumbler, add ice. Serve with straws. Decorate with a strawberry and cherry.

27th Rum Cooler

1 teaspoonful of sugar syrup
¼ gill of lime juice
½ gill of white rum
⅓ pint of soda water

Place a lump of ice in a tumbler, add ingredients, stir well. Serve with a slice of lime.

28th Bacardi Crusta

1 teaspoonful of sugar syrup
⅙ gill of lemon juice
2 dashes of Angostura bitters
1 teaspoonful of pernod
⅓ gill of bacardi rum

Make in a shaker half-filled with broken ice. Place a spiral of lemon rind in a frosted crusta (small wine) glass, add ice and strained cocktail.
    To frost the glass: moisten edges with lemon juice then dip rim in castor sugar.

29th Piña Colada

¾ gill of white rum
1 gill of pineapple juice
½ gill coconut cream

Blend the ingredients with two scoops of crushed ice. Serve in an ice-filled pineapple shell or large glass. Garnish with fruit and parasols.

30th Scorpion

⅛ gill of brandy
½ gill of white rum
⅛ gill of orange juice
1 teaspoonful of orgeat syrup

Use the shaker. Strain into a bowl-shaped glass, half-filled with crushed ice. Garnish with a fresh flower.

31st Casablanca

⅜ gill of white rum
½ gill of pineapple juice
¼ gill of coconut cream
2 dashes of grenadine

Use the shaker. Serve in a large wine glass and garnish with a cherry, a slice of orange and a slice of pineapple.

From left: Spring Shake-Up, Cuba Libre Cocktail, Piña Colada, Scorpion, Casablanca, Bacardi Crusta, Rum Cooler.

VODKA

1st Boo Boo's Special

⅓ gill of orange juice
⅓ gill of pineapple juice
Little lemon juice
1 dash of Angostura bitters
1 dash of grenadine

Use the shaker. Serve in a tumbler garnished with slices of pineapple and orange.

April Fool's Day – all pranks to be played before noon!

2nd Bloody Mary

⅓ gill of vodka
2 dashes of Worcester sauce
Little lemon juice
Tomato juice

Use a 6 oz. goblet. Add ice, vodka, Worcester sauce, a little lemon juice. Top with tomato juice and stir with a stick of celery.

3rd Sandmartin Cocktail

1 teaspoonful of green Chartreuse
¼ gill of Italian vermouth
¼ gill of dry gin

Use the mixing glass. Serve with a little lemon-peel juice squeezed on top.

4th Balalaika Cocktail

⅙ gill of vodka
⅙ gill of Cointreau
⅙ gill of lemon juice

Use the shaker.

5th Dandy Cocktail

1 dash of Angostura bitters
3 dashes of Cointreau
1 piece of lemon peel
1 piece of orange peel
¼ gill of Dubonnet
¼ gill of Canadian Club whisky

Use the shaker.

6th Screwdriver Cocktail

⅓ gill of vodka
⅓ gill of orange juice

Serve with ice in a frosted glass. Decorate with a slice of orange.

To frost the glass: moisten rim of glass with orange juice, then dip in castor sugar.

7th Vodkatini Cocktail

⅓ gill of vodka
⅙ gill of dry vermouth
twist of lemon peel

Use the mixing glass.

 Clockwise from left: Dandy Cocktail, Vodkatini Cocktail, Balalaika Cocktail, Sandmartin Cocktail, Boo Boo's Special, Screwdriver Cocktail, Bloody Mary.

CAMPARI

8th S.W.1 Cocktail

⅙ gill of vodka
⅙ gill of Campari
⅙ gill of orange juice
egg white

Use the shaker. Serve with cocktail cherries.

Campari is an Italian bitter, dark red in colour. Bitters are a perfect apéritif for stimulating the appetitte.

9th Bacardi Cocktail

⅙ gill of fresh lime juice
⅙ gill of bacardi rum
Sugar syrup to taste

Use the shaker. Serve with a slice of lime.

10th Americano Cocktail

⅙ gill of Campari
⅙ gill of sweet vermouth

Stir and fill with soda. Serve with ice.

11th Ladies' Cocktail

2 dashes of Angostura bitters
2 dashes of pernod
2 dashes of anisette
½ gill of Canadian Club whisky

Use the mixing glass. Serve with a slice of pineapple on top.

12th Negroni Cocktail

⅙ gill of dry gin
⅙ gill of sweet vermouth
⅙ gill of Campari

Stir. Serve with ice and ½ slice of orange.

13th Tropical Dawn

¼ gill of gin
¼ gill of fresh orange juice
⅛ gill of Campari

Half-fill the shaker with crushed ice. Add the gin and orange juice. Shake. Pour

into a glass. Pour the Campari over the top. Decorate with a slice of orange and cherries.

14th Fallen Angel Cocktail

1 dash of Angostura bitters
2 dashes of crème de menthe
The juice of half a lemon
½ gill of dry gin

Use the shaker.

 From left: Americano Cocktail, Fallen Angel Cocktail, Bacardi Cocktail, Negroni Cocktail, Ladies' Cocktail, Tropical Dawn, S.W.1 Cocktail.

APRIL

BLUE CURAÇAO

15th Breakfast Egg Nogg

1 egg
¼ gill of blue curaçao
¾ gill of brandy
1 gill of milk

Prepare in a shaker, half-filled with broken ice. Strain into a glass, sprinkle with grated nutmeg. Stir in more milk if desired.

* If a creamier consistency is preferred use cream instead of milk, or a mixture of milk and cream.

This orange flavoured liquer may be obtained in several colours – orange, blue, green or white – all identical in taste.

16th Blue Bird Cocktail

4 dashes of Angostura bitters
5 dashes of blue curaçao
½ gill of dry gin

Use the shaker. Serve with a cherry and a little lemon-peel juice squeezed on top.

17th Bosom Caresser Cocktail

3 dashes of grenadine
The yolk of one egg
⅙ gill of blue curaçao
⅓ gill of brandy

Use the shaker.

18th True Blue

½ gill of blue curaçao
¼ gill of lime juice
Soda water

Serve in a tumbler with a few lumps of ice. Serve with a spiral of lime.

19th Millionaire Cocktail (1)

The white of an egg
2 dashes of blue curaçao
⅙ gill of grenadine
⅓ gill of Canadian Club whisky

Use the shaker.

20th Blue Sour

½ gill of blue curaçao
The juice of half a lemon
1 teaspoonful of sugar syrup

Put ingredients in a shaker, half-filled with broken ice. Shake. Strain into a frosted glass.

To frost the glass: Moisten rim with the curaçao, then dip in castor sugar.

21st East India Cocktail

2 dashes of Angostura bitters
2 dashes of pineapple juice
2 dashes of blue curaçao
½ gill of brandy

Use the shaker. Serve with a cherry and a little lemon-peel juice squeezed on top.

 Clockwise from left: Blue Bird Cocktail, Blue Sour, East India Cocktail, True Blue, Millionaire Cocktail, Breakfast Egg Nog, Bosom Caresser Cocktail (centre).

GALLIANO

22nd Harvey Wallbanger Cocktail

⅓ gill of vodka
⅔ gill of orange juice

Shake and strain onto ice.
Float 2 teaspoons Galliano
liqueur. Serve with straws.

Galliano was named
after a famous 19th
century Italian Major of
the same name. It is a
herbal liqueur,
produced in Milan.

23rd Old Pal Cocktail

⅙ gill of French vermouth
⅙ gill of Campari
⅙ gill of Canadian Club whisky

Use the mixing glass.

St George's Day –
Patron Saint of
England.

24th Golden Dream Cocktail

⅓ gill of Galliano
1/10 gill of Cointreau
1/10 gill of orange juice
1/10 gill of fresh double cream

Shake and serve in
champagne glass.

25th Manhattan Cocktail (dry)

2 dashes of Angostura bitters
¼ gill of French vermouth
¼ gill of Canadian Club whisky

Use the mixing glass. Serve
with an olive or cherry and a

little lemon-peel juice
squeezed on top.

26th Bacardi Special Cocktail

1 teaspoonful of grenadine
The juice of half a lime
⅙ gill of dry gin
⅓ gill of bacardi rum

Use the shaker. Serve with a
slice of lime.

27th Sidecar Cocktail

⅙ gill of fresh lemon juice
⅙ gill of Cointreau
⅙ gill of brandy

Use the shaker.

28th Ink Street Cocktail

⅙ gill of fresh lemon juice
⅙ gill of fresh orange juice
⅙ gill of Canadian Club whisky

Use the shaker. Serve with a
slice of orange and lemon.

Clockwise from top left: Old Pal Cocktail, Manhattan Cocktail, Golden Dream Cocktail, Harvey Wallbanger Cocktail, Sidecar Cocktail, Ink Street Cocktail, Bacardi Special Cocktail.

APRIL/MAY

APRICOT BRANDY

Your Own Special Occasions and Cocktail Ratings

29th Fairy Belle Cocktail

1 teaspoonful of grenadine
The white of one egg
⅛ gill of apricot brandy
⅜ gill of dry gin

Use the shaker.

30th Cuban Cocktail

⅛ gill of fresh lime juice
⅛ gill of apricot brandy
¼ gill of brandy

Using the mixing glass.
Serve with a slice of lime.

1st Champagne Cobbler

3 or 4 dashes of sugar syrup
1 or 2 dashes of lemon juice
2 dashes of old brandy
1 gill of champagne

Prepare in the mixing glass (*not* the shaker), half-filled with broken ice. Stir gently, and strain into a tumbler half-full of broken ice. Decorate with fruit, and serve with a straw.

2nd Paradise Cocktail

⅙ gill of fresh orange juice
⅙ gill of apricot brandy
⅙ gill of dry gin

Use the shaker. Serve with a slice of orange.

3rd Piccadilly Cocktail

1 dash of pernod
1 dash of grenadine
⅙ gill of French vermouth
⅓ gill of dry gin

Use the shaker.

4th Gin Daisy

⅛ gill of grenadine
½ gill of lemon juice
½ gill of dry gin

Shake well, and strain into an ice-filled tumbler. Top up with soda water. Stir and decorate with fruit. Alternative serving: Strain into an ice-filled wine glass, omit soda water. Decorate with fruit. Half quantities for this method.

5th Fourth Degree Cocktail

4 dashes of pernod
⅛ gill of French vermouth
⅛ gill of Italian vermouth
¼ gill of dry gin

Use the mixing glass. Serve with a cherry.

44

*From left: Cuban Cocktail, Fairy Belle Cocktail, Champagne Cobbler,
Paradise Cocktail, Piccadilly Cocktail, Fourth Degree Cocktail, Gin Daisy.*

MAY

CHERRY BRANDY

MAY

CHERRY BRANDY

MAY

CHERRY BRANDY

6th Singapore Sling

⅙ gill of lemon juice
⅓ gill of gin
⅙ gill of cherry brandy

Put the ingredients in a shaker, half-filled with broken ice. Shake well, and strain into an ice-filled tumbler. Fill up with soda water and stir. Serve with a slice of orange, cherries and a parasol.

This drink originated from Raffles Hotel in Singapore.

7th Brandy Fix

1 teaspoonful of sugar syrup
The juice of half a lemon
¼ gill of brandy
¼ gill of cherry brandy
A little water to taste

Place ingredients in a tumbler, stir. Fill up glass with crushed ice. Decorate with fruit and serve with straws.

8th Brandy Smash

½ lump of sugar
4 sprigs of fresh mint
½ gill of brandy

In the shaker dissolve the sugar in a little water (or soda water). Add the sprigs of mint, muddle slightly, then remove them. Half-fill the shaker with ice and add brandy. Shake well, then strain into a wine glass. Stir, decorate with a sprig of mint or fruit, and serve with straws.

9th Blood and Sand Cocktail

⅛ gill of fresh orange juice
⅛ gill of Italian vermouth
⅛ gill of cherry brandy
⅛ gill of Scotch whisky

Use the mixing glass. Serve with a slice of orange and a cherry.

10th London Cocktail

2 dashes of orange bitters
2 dashes of sugar syrup
2 dashes of pernod
½ gill of dry gin

Use the mixing glass. Serve with olives and a little lemon-peel juice squeezed on top.

11th Vanderbilt Cocktail

2 dashes of Angostura bitters
3 dashes of sugar syrup
⅛ gill of cherry brandy
⅛ gill of brandy

Use the mixing glass.

12th Cooperstown Cocktail

⅙ gill of French vermouth
⅙ gill of Italian vermouth
⅙ gill of dry gin
2 sprigs of fresh mint

Use the mixing glass. Serve with a cherry on top.

Top from left: Blood and Sand Cocktail, Brandy Fix, Singapore Sling, Brandy Smash. Bottom from left: Cooperstown Cocktail, London Cocktail, Vanderbilt Cocktail.

MAY

SWEDISH PUNCH

13th Waldorf Cocktail

The juice of half a lime or a
quarter of a lemon
⅙ gill of dry gin
⅓ gill of Swedish punch

Use the mixing glass.

Swedish Punch is a
blend of rum, aquavir
(Schnapps), wine and
syrup. Delicious served
either hot or cold or in
cocktails.

14th Doctor Cocktail

⅓ gill of Swedish punch
⅙ gill of fresh lime juice (or
lemon juice)

Use the shaker.

Better than any
prescription!

15th Boomerang Cocktail

1 dash of Angostura bitters
1 dash of fresh lemon juice
⅙ gill of French (or dry
Martini) vermouth

⅙ gill of Swedish punch
⅙ gill of Canadian Club whisky

Use the shaker.

16th Tanglefoot Cocktail

For four persons:
⅓ gill of fresh lemon juice
⅓ gill of fresh orange juice

⅔ gill of Swedish punch
⅔ gill of bacardi rum

Use the shaker. Serve with a
slice of orange.

17th Melba Cocktail

2 dashes of pernod
The juice of half a lime or a
quarter of a lemon

2 dashes of grenadine
¼ gill of Swedish punch
¼ gill of bacardi rum

Use the shaker. Serve with a
slice of lime and lemon and
a cherry.

18th Fair and Warmer Cocktail

2 dashes of blue curaçao
⅙ gill of Italian vermouth
⅓ gill of bacardi rum

Use the mixing glass. Serve
with a cherry.

19th Greenbriar Cocktail

1 dash of peach bitters
⅓ gill of dry sherry
⅙ gill of French vermouth
1 sprig of fresh mint

Use the mixing glass.

From left: Waldorf Cocktail, Greenbriar Cocktail, Fair and Warmer Cocktail, Tanglefoot Cocktail, Melba Cocktail, Doctor Cocktail, Boomerang Cocktail.

CALVADOS

20th Bentley Cocktail

¼ gill of Dubonnet
¼ gill of calvados

Use the shaker. Serve with a cherry.

21st Twelve Miles Out Cocktail

⅙ gill of bacardi rum
⅙ gill of Swedish punch
⅙ gill of calvados

Use the mixing glass. Serve with a little lemon-peel juice squeezed on top and a slice of lemon.

22nd Star Cocktail

1 dash of French vermouth
1 dash of Italian vermouth
1 teaspoonful of fresh grapefruit juice

¼ gill of calvados
¼ gill of dry gin

Use the shaker. Serve with slices of apple.

23rd Tipperary Cocktail

3 dashes of grenadine
1 teaspoonful of fresh orange juice
⅙ gill of Italian vermouth
⅓ gill of dry gin

Use the shaker. Serve with sprigs of mint.

24th Angel Face Cocktail

⅙ gill of apricot brandy
⅙ gill of calvados
⅙ gill of dry gin

Use the shaker.

25th Ginger Ale Cup (non-alcoholic)

½ lb. of loaf sugar
1 quart of boiling water
½ teacupful of lime juice
1 bottle of ginger ale, preferably chilled

Dissolve sugar in the boiling water, chill. Place a large piece of ice in a glass jug or bowl, add ingredients, and stir well. Decorate with sprigs of fresh mint and fresh fruit. Serve immediately. Serves 4.

26th Prince's Smile Cocktail

1 dash of fresh lemon juice
⅛ gill of apricot brandy
⅛ gill of calvados
¼ gill of dry gin

Use the shaker. Serve with a slice of lemon.

Clockwise from top left: Tipperary Cocktail, Bentley Cocktail, Star Cocktail, Prince's Smile Cocktail, Angel Face Cocktail, Ginger Ale Cup, Twelve Miles Out Cocktail.

ORANGE OR BROWN CURAÇAO

27th Rum Daisy

⅛ gill of grenadine
½ gill of lemon juice
2 or 3 dashes brown or orange
    curaçao
½ gill of white rum

Shake well, and strain into an ice-filled tumbler. Top up with soda water. Stir and decorate with fruit. Alternative serving: Strain

into an ice-filled wine glass, omit soda water. Decorate with fruit. Half quantities for this method.

28th Roulette Cocktail

⅛ gill of bacardi rum
⅛ gill of Swedish punch
¼ gill of calvados

Use the mixing glass.

29th New York Cocktail

1 lump of sugar
The juice of one lime or half a
    lemon

2 dashes of grenadine
1 piece of orange peel
½ gill of Canadian Club whisky

Use the shaker. Serve with a little lemon-peel juice squeezed on top.

30th Rye Fizz

5 or 6 dashes of grenadine
¾ gill of lemon juice
The white of an egg

1 teaspoonful of brown or orange
    curaçao
½ gill of Canadian Club whisky

Use a shaker, strain into a highball glass, add ice. Top up with soda water if desired. Serve with straws.

31st Claridge Cocktail

1/12 gill of apricot brandy
1/12 gill of Cointreau
⅙ gill of French vermouth
⅙ gill of dry gin

Use the shaker. Serve with a cherry.

1st Whisky Daisy

⅙ gill of grenadine
½ gill of lemon juice
½ gill of lime juice
¼ gill of orange juice
½ gill of Scotch whisky

Shake well, and strain. The flavour may be considered improved if two dashes of brown curaçao are added. Serve in an ice-filled tumbler. Top up with soda

water. Stir and decorate with fruit.
Alternative serving: Strain into an ice-filled wine glass. Omit soda. Decorate with fruit. Half quantities for this method.

2nd White Cocktail

2 dashes of orange bitters
6 dashes of anisette, or pernod
    and dash of sugar syrup
½ gill of dry gin

Use the mixing glass. Serve with lemon-peel juice squeezed on top.

 From left; Roulette Cocktail, Rye Fizz, New York Cocktail, Whisky Daisy, Claridge Cocktail, Rum Daisy, White Cocktail.

JUNE

CRÈME DE CASSIS/PORT

3rd Kir Cocktail

1 glass of dry white wine, chilled
1 teaspoonful of crème de cassis

With a teaspoon, float crème de cassis on the wine.

Cassis is a brandy-based blackcurrant liquer. It is a great way of making a cheap wine very drinkable.

4th Calvados Cocktail

For four persons:
⅔ gill of fresh orange juice
⅓ gill of Cointreau
⅓ gill of orange bitters
⅔ gill of calvados

Use the shaker. Serve with a slice of orange and apple.

5th Parisian Cocktail

⅙ gill of French vermouth
⅙ gill of crème de cassis
⅙ gill of dry gin

Use the mixing glass. Serve in a frosted glass if desired. To frost the glass: moisten the rim with crème de cassis then dip in castor sugar.

6th Dempsey Cocktail

2 dashes of pernod
3 dashes of grenadine
⅓ gill of calvados
⅙ gill of dry gin

Use the shaker. Serve with cherries.

7th Port Wine Sangaree

1 teaspoonful of sugar
½ gill of water
1 gill of port

Dissolve sugar in water in a tumbler, add port and fill with crushed ice. Stir well, decorate with grated nutmeg and fruit if desired.

Ruby Port is ideal for cocktails, and is a good keeper.

8th Roosevelt Cocktail

⅙ gill of gin
⅙ gill of white rum
⅙ gill of lemon juice
⅙ gill of grenadine

Use the shaker.

9th Port Wine Cocktail

1 dash of brandy
½ gill of port

Use the mixing glass. Serve with a little orange-peel juice squeezed on top and a slice of orange.

From left: Roosevelt Cocktail, Parisian Cocktail, Port Wine Cocktail, Kir Cocktail, Dempsey Cocktail, Calvados Cocktail, Port Wine Sangaree.

JUNE

JUNE | Your Own Special Occasions and Cocktail Ratings

	Your Own Special Occasions and Cocktail Ratings

10th Hawaiian Cocktail

⅓ gill of dry gin
⅓ gill of orange juice
1 dash Cointreau

Shake.

11th Mississippi Mule Cocktail

For four persons:
⅓ gill of fresh lemon juice
⅓ gill of crème de cassis
1⅓ gills of dry gin

Use the shaker.

12th Grapefruit Cocktail (1)

1 grapefruit
1 small tin of pineapple chunks
2 bananas
1 gill of sherry

Remove the peel, pulp and pips from the grapefruit, and press it through a sieve. Slice the bananas and pineapple thinly, then add them to the grapefruit purée, in equal quantities, making one pint altogether. Sprinkle castor sugar on the fruit, and pour the sherry over it. Stand on ice for about an hour. Serve in sherbet glasses.

13th Cassis Highball

⅙ gill of crème de cassis
⅙ gill of dry gin
sparkling apple juice

Use the mixing glass for the gin and crème de cassis. Serve in a tumbler with a few lumps of ice and fill up with apple juice. Decorate with a slice of apple.

A very refreshing drink as the days become warmer.

14th Pineapple Lemonade

1 small tin of pineapple chunks
2 lemons
¼ lb. of loaf sugar

Remove the rind from the lemons, without any white pith, and put it in a jug. Add one pint of boiling water, the syrup from the tin of pineapple, and the pineapple cut very small or liquidised in its syrup. Squeeze the juice from the lemons, mix it with the sugar, and add to the jug. Strain. Add soda water and ice.

15th Iced Tea

Make the tea in the usual way, allowing one teaspoonful of tea to half a pint of water. Allow it to draw, then strain and leave to cool. Add a little sugar if desired, and some slices of lemon or fresh fruit juice: then stand on ice until required. Serve with small ice cubes.

Take a fresh look at tea – some say its the best drink in the world!

16th Grape Cocktail

1 dash of Angostura bitters
¼ gill of grape juice
½ gill of sugar syrup
Fresh fruit: grapes, oranges, lemons, strawberries.
1 gill of soda water

Use the mixing glass, half-filled with broken ice. Add the Angostura bitters, then the grape juice and sugar syrup. Stir well, and strain into a tumbler. Fill up with soda water, and serve with fresh fruit on top.

56

 Clockwise from top left: Mississippi Mule Cocktail, Grape Cocktail, Pineapple Lemonade, Hawaiian Cocktail, Cassis Highball, Iced Tea, Grapefruit Cocktail (1).

JUNE

PLYMOUTH GIN

17ᵗʰ Pink Gin Cocktail

1 dash of Angostura bitters
½ gill of Plymouth Gin

Use the shaker.

Plymouth Gin is unsweetened and the correct gin to use for a pink gin, the traditional gin of the British Royal Navy.

18ᵗʰ Gin Fix

2 teaspoonfuls of sugar syrup
The juice of half a lemon
¾ gill of dry gin
Water to taste

Place ingredients in a tumbler, stir. Fill up glass with crushed ice. Decorate with fruit and serve with straws.

19ᵗʰ Bijou Cocktail

1 dash of orange bitters
⅙ gill of Plymouth gin
⅙ gill of green Chartreuse
⅙ gill of Italian vermouth

Use the mixing glass. Serve with a cherry and a little lemon-peel juice squeezed on top.

20ᵗʰ 'S.G.' Cocktail

3 dashes of grenadine
⅙ gill of fresh lemon juice
⅙ gill of fresh orange juice
⅙ gill of Canadian Club whisky

Use the shaker.

21ˢᵗ Champagne Julep

1 lump of sugar
2 sprigs of fresh mint
Chilled champagne

Put sugar in a champagne glass, add sprigs of mint and gently crush leaves with a spoon. Fill with champagne. Stir gently. Decorate with seasonal fruit and mint.

Longest day and shortest night of the year (in the northern hemisphere.) A good excuse to crack open the champagne.

22ⁿᵈ Olivette Cocktail

3 dashes of pernod
2 dashes of orange bitters
2 dashes of sugar syrup
½ gill of Plymouth gin

Use the mixing glass. Serve with an olive and a little lemon-peel juice squeezed on top.

23ʳᵈ Depth Charge Cocktail

4 dashes of fresh lemon juice
2 dashes of grenadine
¼ gill of calvados
¼ gill of brandy

Use the shaker.

 From left: 'S.G.' Cocktail, Bijou Cocktail, Gin Fix, Depth Charge Cocktail, Pink Gin Cocktail, Champagne Julep, Olivette Cocktail.

JUNE

TEQUILA

24ᵗʰ Tequila Sunrise Cocktail

⅓ gill of tequila
⅔ gill of orange juice
dash of grenadine

Shake well. Pour into the glass. Add dash of grenadine. Serve with straws.

Midsummer's Day

25ᵗʰ Brandy Julep

1 teaspoonful of castor sugar
4 tender sprigs of fresh mint
¾ gill of brandy

Cover mint with sugar in a tumbler or tankard. Add just enough water to dissolve the sugar. Crush mint gently.

Add brandy and fill glass with broken ice. Stir. Decorate with mint and fruit.

26ᵗʰ Margarita Cocktail

⅓ gill of tequila
⅓ gill of lemon juice (fresh)
⅙ gill of Cointreau

Shake. Frost rim of glass with salt.

27ᵗʰ Strawberry Cream Cooler

½ gill of gin
¼ gill of lemon juice
¾ gill of cream
3 strawberries
1 teaspoonful of sugar

Blend for a few seconds. Pour into a tumbler and add soda water and ice cubes. Garnish with strawberries.

28ᵗʰ American Beauty Cocktail

1 dash of crème de menthe
⅛ gill of fresh orange juice
⅛ gill of grenadine

⅛ gill of French vermouth
⅛ gill of brandy
dash of port

Use the shaker. Serve with a little port wine on top, and a slice of orange.

29ᵗʰ Strawberry Dawn

⅓ gill of gin
⅓ gill of coconut cream
3 fresh strawberries
2 scoops of crushed ice

Blend for a few seconds. Serve in a large glass.

30ᵗʰ Bloodhound Cocktail

3 crushed strawberries
⅛ gill of French vermouth
⅛ gill of Italian vermouth
¼ gill of dry gin

Use the shaker. Serve with a strawberry.

 From left: Strawberry Dawn, Bloodhound Cocktail, Tequila Sunrise, Margarita Cocktail, Strawberry Cream Cooler, American Beauty Cocktail, Brandy Julep Cocktail.

CRÈME DE BANANE

1st Banana Daiquiri

½ gill of white rum
¼ gill of crème de banane
The juice of half a lime
Half a banana

Blend for a few seconds with
two scoops of crushed ice.
Serve in a large wine glass.

2nd Cherry Blossom Cocktail

1 dash of grenadine
1 dash of orange curaçao
1 dash of fresh lemon juice

¼ gill of cherry brandy
¼ gill of brandy

Use the shaker. Serve very
cold, with a fresh cherry.

3rd Barracuda

½ gill of white rum
¼ gill of Galliano
½ gill of pineapple juice

2 dashes of sugar syrup
Juice of half a lime
Champagne

Use the shaker for all the
ingredients except the
champagne. Serve in a
pineapple shell and top with
champagne.

4th Banana Bliss

¼ gill of crème de banane
¼ gill of white rum
¼ gill of cream

⅛ gill of orange juice
1 dash of Angostura bitters
3–5 drops of grenadine

Use the shaker for all the
ingredients except the
grenadine. Strain into a
tumbler. Add the grenadine.

5th Commodore Cocktail

3 dashes of orange bitters
3 dashes of sugar syrup
The juice of half a lime or a
    quarter of a lemon
½ gill of Canadian Club whisky

Use the shaker. Serve with a
slice of lemon and lime.

You needn't be on the
sea to enjoy these
cocktails!

6th Hot Deck Cocktail

1 dash of Jamaica ginger
⅛ gill of Italian vermouth
⅜ gill of Canadian Club whisky

Use the mixing glass.

7th Quarter Deck Cocktail

1 teaspoonful of lime juice
⅙ gill of dry sherry
⅓ gill of rum

Use the mixing glass.

 Clockwise from bottom left: Commodore Cocktail, Banana Daiquiri, Cherry Blossom Cocktail, Barracuda, Quarter Deck Cocktail, Banana Bliss, Hot Deck.

APPLEJACK BRANDY

8th Third Rail Cocktail

1 dash of pernod
⅙ gill of calvados
⅙ gill of brandy
⅙ gill of bacardi rum

Use the shaker.

Applejack brandy is produced in New England from the fermented mash of cider apples, then matured in wood for at least 2 years.

9th Shandy Gaff

½ pint of ale, chilled
½ pint of ginger ale, chilled

Mix in a tumbler and serve ice cold, decorated with fruit.

10th Applejack Sour

2 dashes of sugar syrup
1 dash of grenadine
The juice of half a lemon (or equal parts of lemon and lime)

½ gill of applejack brandy or calvados

Mix in a shaker, half-filled with broken ice. Strain into a small wine glass or cocktail glass. If desired, add a little soda water, and decorate with apple slices.

11th Applejack Rabbit Cocktail

For four persons:
⅓ gill of fresh lemon juice
⅓ gill of fresh orange juice

⅔ gill of maple syrup
⅔ gill of applejack brandy

Use the shaker. Serve with slices of orange and lemon and a cherry.

12th Sundew Cocktail

1 dash of Angostura bitters
¼ gill of sugar syrup
¼ gill of grape juice
½ gill of orange juice

2 slices of orange
¾ gill of soda water

Use the mixing glass. Add the Angostura bitters, then the sugar syrup, orange juice and grape juice. Stir well, and strain into a glass. Fill up with soda water, and serve with slices of orange and grapes on top.

13th Applejack Highball

¾ gill of Applejack brandy
Soda water or ginger ale

Pour into a tumbler with a few lumps of ice. Serve with a piece of lemon peel or a slice of lemon.

14th Jack Rose Cocktail

The juice of one lime or half a lemon
⅛ gill of grenadine
⅜ gill of applejack brandy or calvados

Use the shaker.

 Clockwise from bottom left: Shandy Gaff, Applejack Highball, Applejack Rabbit Cocktail, Sundew Cocktail, Jack Rose Cocktail, Applejack Sour, Third Rail Cocktail (centre).

JULY

15th Iced Chocolate

1 pint of chocolate
Vanilla ice cream

Make the chocolate in the normal way, and allow it to cool, then stand in a jug surrounded with ice or put in the refrigerator. When required, serve in small glasses topped with vanilla ice cream.

16th Egg Lemonade (non-alcoholic)

The juice of one lemon
1 oz of castor sugar
1 egg
Ice

Prepare in the mixing glass, stir well, and strain into a tumbler. Serve with water or soda water.

17th Mixed Fruit Cocktail

Equal amounts of:
Blackcurrants
Raspberries
Strawberries

Sugar to taste
A little lemon juice

Mash the fruits to a pulp, and add the sugar. Strain the sweetened juice into the shaker, half filled with broken ice, and add the lemon juice and a little water. Shake well, and strain into a wine glass.

Very refreshing and contains lots of vitamin C.

18th Cherry Cocktail

1 dash of Angostura bitters
2 dashes of lime juice
¼ gill of ginger syrup
¼ gill of cherry syrup
2 slices of orange

4 or 5 stoned cherries
1 gill of soda water

Use the mixing glass, half-filled with broken ice. Add the Angostura bitters, then the lime juice, ginger syrup, and cherry syrup. Stir well, and strain into a tumbler. Fill up with soda water, and serve with slices of orange and cherries.

An attractive drink for all ages.

19th Blackcurrant Cocktail

2 teaspoonfuls of powdered sugar
¼ cupful of blackcurrants
½ grapefruit

Cut a hole in the middle of the half-grapefruit, and fill with blackcurrants. Serve with powdered sugar.

20th Raspberry Lemonade

1 lb. of raspberries
2 lemons
¼ lb. of castor sugar

Press the raspberries through a sieve, add the juice of the lemons and the sugar, stir well, and mix with one quart of cold water. Serve with ice, and decorate with raspberries.

When raspberries go out of season, use some from the freezer.

21st Orangeade

4 oranges
2 lemons
2 lb. of loaf sugar

Scrape the rinds from the oranges and lemons by rubbing with the loaf sugar. Put the sugar in a jug, and pour two quarts of boiling water over it. Add the juice of the oranges and lemons, stir well, and allow to cool. Strain and serve with slices of oranges and lemons.

Clockwise from left: Iced Chocolate, Blackcurrant Cocktail, Egg Lemonade, Mixed Fruit Cocktail, Orangeade, Raspberry Lemonade, Cherry Cocktail.

MARASCHINO/YELLOW CHARTREUSE

22nd Allen (special) Cocktail

1 dash of lemon juice
⅙ gill of maraschino
⅓ gill of Plymouth gin

Use the shaker. Serve with a cherry.

Marashino is an Italian liqueur, made with the sour black marasca cherries. The flavour is drier than that of cherry brandy.

23rd Cider Cup (2)

⅓ gill of Cointreau
¼ gill of maraschino
½ gill of brandy
¾ gill of dry sherry

1 teaspoonful of lemon juice
1 quart of cider, preferably chilled

Place a large piece of ice in a glass jug or bowl. Add ingredients, stir well, and decorate with fruit and sprigs of fresh mint. Serve immediately. (Serves 4.)

24th Depth Bomb Cocktail

1 dash of fresh lemon juice
4 dashes of grenadine
¼ gill of calvados
¼ gill of brandy

Use the shaker.

Don't let the name put you off trying this one!

25th Rum Crusta

1 teaspoonful of sugar syrup
⅙ gill of lemon juice
2 dashes of Angostura bitters
1 teaspoonful of maraschino
⅓ gill of white or dark rum

Make in a shaker half-filled with broken ice. Place a spiral of lemon rind in a frosted crusta (small wine) glass, add ice and strained

cocktail. Decorate with seasonal fruit. To frost the glass: moisten edges with lemon juice them dip rim in castor sugar.

26th Yellow Parrot Cocktail

⅙ gill of pernod
⅙ gill of yellow Chartreuse
⅙ gill of apricot brandy

Use the shaker.

Yellow Chartreuse is sweeter and less potent than the green variety. It's made from over 130 types of herbs and spices.

27th Chocolate Cocktail (1)

1 teaspoonful of powdered chocolate
The yolk of one egg
¼ gill of yellow Chartreuse
¼ gill of port

Use the shaker. Serve with a flake chocolate bar.

Try this one after dinner.

28th Golden Slipper – a Pousse Café

The yolk of an egg
⅙ gill of yellow Chartreuse
⅙ gill of brandy

Add ingredients in the stated order, pour liquids over the back of a spoon so that they touch the sides of the glass.

Serve in a pousse café glass. Do not stir, a layered effect should be achieved.

Clockwise from left: Depth Bomb Cocktail, Allen (Special) Cocktail, Yellow Parrot Cocktail, Chocolate Cocktail (1), Golden Slipper, Rum Crusta, Cider Cup (2).

29th Brandy Crusta

1 teaspoonful of sugar syrup
⅙ gill of lemon juice
1 dash of Angostura bitters
1 teaspoonful of maraschino
1 dash of orange bitters
⅓ gill of brandy

Make in a shaker half-filled with broken ice. Place a spiral of orange rind in a frosted crusta (small wine) glass, add ice and strained cocktail. Decorate with seasonal fruit.
To frost the glass: moisten edges with lemon juice then dip rim in castor sugar.

30th Tuxedo Cocktail

1 dash of pernod
1 dash of maraschino
2 dashes of orange bitters

¼ gill of French vermouth
¼ gill of dry gin

Use the mixing glass. Serve with grapes, slices of banana and a little lemon-peel juice squeezed on top.

31st Sherry Sangaree

1 teaspoonful of sugar
½ gill of water
¾ gill of sherry

Dissolve sugar in the water in a tumbler, add sherry and fill with crushed ice. Stir well, decorate with grated nutmeg and cherries.

1st White Rose Cocktail

The juice of quarter of an orange
*The juice of half a lime or a
    quarter of a lemon*

The white of one egg
⅛ gill of maraschino
⅜ gill of dry gin

Use the shaker. Serve with seasonal fruit.

2nd Iced Coffee

*2 gills strong coffee (made with
    freshly-ground coffee)*
sugar to sweeten

2 gills vanilla-flavoured milk
1 gill cream
whipped cream

Sweeten coffee while hot, then chill. Add milk and cream. Chill until required. Serve in glasses topped with whipped cream.

3rd Chocolate Cocktail (2)

*1 teaspoonful of powdered
    chocolate*
1 egg

¼ gill of yellow Chartreuse
¼ gill of maraschino

Use the shaker.

4th Grapefruit Drink

1 grapefruit
3 oranges
¼ lb. of loaf sugar
1 bottle of soda water

Rub the loaf sugar on the rind of the oranges and then put it in a large jug. Pour over it one pint of water, the strained juice of the oranges and of the grapefruit. Strain, add a lump of ice and some soda water to serve.

A drink for any time of the day.

Clockwise from left: Grapefruit Drink, White Rose Cocktail, Chocolate Cocktail, Sherry Sangaree, Tuxedo Cocktail, Iced Coffee, Brandy Crusta (centre).

AUGUST

KUMMEL

5th Green Dragon Cocktail

For four persons:
8 dashes of peach bitters
¼ gill of fresh lemon juice
¼ gill of kummel

½ gill of crème de menthe
1 gill of dry gin

Use the shaker.

Kummel comes mainly from Holland or Germany. This colourless liqueur is flavoured with many herbs and spices including caraway seeds.

6th Hock Cup

¼ gill of kummel
½ gill of brandy
⅓ gill of yellow Chartreuse
¼ gill of maraschino

1 bottle of hock, preferably chilled
1 pint of soda water, preferably chilled

Place a large piece of ice in a glass jug or bowl. Add ingredients, stir well and decorate with fruit. Serve immediately. Serves 4.

The perfect drink when serving a crowd.

7th Silver Streak Cocktail

¼ gill of kummel
¼ gill of dry gin

Use the shaker.

8th Egg Punch (non-alcoholic)

1 egg
1 tablespoonful of vanilla syrup
Ice
Balance of milk and soda water

Beat the egg in a basin, and add vanilla syrup and chopped ice. Shake in the shaker, and strain into a

long glass. Add the milk to three-quarters fill the glass, then fill up with soda water.

9th Diplomat Cocktail

1 dash of maraschino
⅓ gill of French vermouth
⅙ gill of Italian vermouth

Use the mixing glass. Serve with a cherry and a little

lemon-peel juice squeezed on top.

10th Gin Crusta

1 teaspoonful of sugar syrup
⅙ gill of lemon juice
1 dash of Angostura bitters
1 teaspoonful of maraschino or pineapple syrup

1 dash orange bitters
⅓ gill of gin

Make in a shaker half-filled with broken ice. Place a

spiral of orange rind in a frosted crusta (small wine) glass, add ice and strained cocktail.
To frost the glass: moisten edges with lemon juice then dip rim in castor sugar.

11th Sunset Cooler

½ gill of campari
1 gill fresh orange juice

Pour into a tumbler, fill up with ice and stir. Decorate with a slice of orange.

From left: Sunset Cooler, Gin Crusta, Diplomat Cocktail, Green Dragon Cocktail, Silver Streak Cocktail, Egg Punch, Hock Cup.

AUGUST

12th Western Rose Cocktail

1 dash of fresh lemon juice
⅛ gill of French vermouth

⅛ gill of apricot brandy
¼ gill of dry gin

Use the shaker.

13th Inca Cocktail

1 dash of orgeat syrup
1 dash of orange bitters
⅛ gill of dry gin

⅛ gill of dry sherry
⅛ gill of French vermouth
⅛ gill of Italian vermouth

Use the mixing glass.
Decorate with a slice of
orange.

14th Porto Fraise

½ gill of port
*⅙ gill of fraisette (strawberry
syrup)*

Mix and serve in the same
glass, add water or soda
water and a lump of ice. Stir
and serve.

* As an alternative to port
use French vermouth.

15th Salty Dog

½ gill of vodka
1 gill of grapefruit juice

Pour ingredients into an ice-
filled, salt-frosted glass and
stir.

To frost the glass: moisten
edges with lemon juice then
dip into salt.

16th Kir Royale

2 dashes of crème de cassis
chilled champagne

Serve in a champagne glass,
stir carefully.

A very special Kir.

17th Club Cocktail

*1 or 2 dashes of Angostura
bitters*
3 dashes of grenadine
½ gill of Canadian Club whisky

Use the mixing glass. Serve
with a cherry and a little

lemon-peel juice squeezed on
top.

18th Brandy Cobbler

1 teaspoonful of sugar syrup
1 teaspoonful of brown curaçao
1 gill of brandy

Shake or mix well, and
strain into a tumbler half-full
of broken ice. Decorate with

slices of orange or lemon,
and a sprig of mint. Serve
with a straw.

Clockwise from bottom left: Western Rose Cocktail, Inca Cocktail, Kir Royale, Brandy Cobbler, Salty Dog, Club Cocktail, Porto Fraise.

AMER PICON

19th Brooklyn Cocktail

1 dash of Amer Picon
1 dash of maraschino
*⅙ gill of French (or dry
   Martini) vermouth*
⅓ gill of Canadian Club whisky

Use the mixing glass. Serve
with a cherry.

Amer Picon is a French
aromatized wine with a
slightly bitter flavour.

20th Whisky Sour

1 teaspoonful of sugar syrup
The juice of half a lemon
½ gill of Scotch whisky

Mix in a shaker, half-filled
with broken ice. Strain into
a small wine glass. If

desired, add a little soda
water, and decorate with a
slice of lemon.

21st Picon Cocktail

¼ gill of Italian vermouth
¼ gill of Amer Picon

Use the mixing glass.
Decorate with a slice of
orange.

A good appetiser.

22nd Oppenheim Cocktail

⅛ gill of grenadine
⅛ gill of Italian vermouth
¼ gill of Scotch whisky

Use the mixing glass.

23rd Pegu Club Cocktail

1 dash of Angostura bitters
1 dash of orange bitters
3 dashes of lime juice

⅙ gill of Cointreau
⅓ gill of dry gin

Use the mixing glass. Serve
with a piece of orange.

24th Grapefruit Cocktail (2)

½ grapefruit
1 orange
Slices of banana

*1 tablespoon of sherry or white
   wine*
The juice of one lemon

Peel the grapefruit and
orange, and break both fruits
into sections. Arrange round
sides of a sherbet glass. Add
slices of banana. Sprinkle
with icing sugar, squeeze
over the lemon juice and
pour over the sherry or wine.

A dessert cocktail.

25th Silver Fizz

1 teaspoonful of sugar syrup
*The juice of one lemon, or equal
   parts of lemon and lime*
The white of one egg
¾ gill of dry gin

Use a shaker, strain into a
highball glass, add ice. Top
with soda water, stir. Serve
with straws and slices of
lemon and/or lime.

 From left: Whisky Sour, Brooklyn Cocktail, Pegu Club Cocktail, Oppenheim Cocktail, Silver Fizz, Picon Cocktail, Grapefruit Cocktail (2).

BÉNÉDICTINE

26th 'Oh, Henry!' Cocktail

⅙ gill of ginger ale
⅙ gill of Bénédictine
⅙ gill of Scotch whisky

Use the mixing glass.

Bénédictine could be one of the oldest liquers in the world. It originated in Fécamp, Normandy where it was produced by the Bénédictine monks.

27th Fioupe Cocktail

1 teaspoonful of Bénédictine
¼ gill of Italian vermouth
¼ gill of brandy

Use the mixing glass. Serve with a cherry and a little

lemon-peel juice squeezed on top.

28th Creole Cocktail

2 dashes of Amer Picon
2 dashes of Bénédictine
¼ gill of Italian vermouth
¼ gill of Canadian Club whisky

Use the mixing glass. Serve with a little lemon-peel juice squeezed on top.

29th Straits Sling

The juice of half a lemon
2 dashes of Angostura bitters
2 dashes of orange bitters
⅛ gill of cherry brandy

⅛ gill of Bénédictine
½ gill of dry gin
Put the ingredients in the shaker, half-filled with

broken ice. Shake well, and strain into an ice-filled tumbler. Fill up with soda water, and stir. Serve with a cherry and slices of orange and lemon.

30th Cardinale Cocktail

⅕ gill of dry gin
¹⁄₁₀ gill of French vermouth (dry)
¹⁄₁₀ gill of Campari

Shake and strain into cocktail glass.

31st Oriental Cocktail

The juice of half a lime
⅛ gill of Cointreau
⅛ gill of Italian vermouth
¼ gill of Canadian Club whisky

Use the shaker.

1st Whisky Rickey

The juice of half a lime
¾ gill of Scotch whisky

Mix in a tumbler with a lump of ice. Fill up with

soda water, and stir well. Serve with a slice of lime.

From left: Straits Sling, Cardinale Cocktail, Whisky Rickey, Oriental Cocktail, Creole Cocktail, Fioupe Cocktail, 'Oh Henry!' Cocktail.

SEPTEMBER

SLOE GIN

2nd **Sloe Gin Cocktail**

⅛ gill of French vermouth
⅛ gill of Italian vermouth
¼ gill of sloe gin

Use the mixing glass.

Sloe Gin is a sweet red liqueur, made by soaking sloe berries in gin.

3rd **Applejack Rickey**

The juice of half a lime
¾ gill of applejack brandy

Mix in a tumbler with a lump of ice. Fill up with soda water, stir well.

4th **Blackthorn Cocktail**

2 dashes of orange bitters
⅙ gill of Italian vermouth
⅙ gill of French vermouth
⅙ gill of sloe gin

Use the mixing glass. Serve with a cherry and a little lemon-peel juice squeezed on top.

Sloe berries are the fruit of the blackthorn shrub – try making some sloe gin this autumn – though the best sloe gin is matured for 10 years!

5th **Planter's Cocktail**

⅛ gill of fresh lime juice (or lemon juice)
⅛ gill of sugar syrup
¼ gill of white rum

Use the mixing glass. Serve with a slice of lime.

6th **Opening Cocktail**

⅛ gill of grenadine
⅛ gill of Italian vermouth
¼ gill of Canadian Club whisky

Use the mixing glass.

A perfect beginning to an evening.

7th **Burgundy Cup**

1 bottle of burgundy, preferably chilled
½ gill of brandy
½ gill of maraschino

¼ gill of brown curaçao
2 or 3 dashes of Bénédictine
1 bottle of soda water, preferably chilled

Place a large piece of ice in a glass jug or bowl. Add ingredients, stir well, decorate with fruit and serve immediately. Serves 4.

Only wine and soda to purchase – other ingredients have been accumulated over the previous months.

8th **One Exciting Night Cocktail**

1 dash of orange juice
⅙ gill of French vermouth
⅙ gill of Italian vermouth
⅙ gill Plymouth gin

Use the shaker. Serve with a little lemon-peel juice squeezed on top.

From top left: Planter's Cocktail, Blackthorn Cocktail, One Exciting Night Cocktail, Applejack Rickey, Burgundy Cup, Opening Cocktail, Sloe Gin Cocktail.

FERNET BRANCA

9th King Cole Cocktail

1 dash of Fernet Branca
2 dashes of sugar syrup
½ gill of Scotch whisky

Use the mixing glass.
Decorate with slices of
orange and pineapple.

10th Port Cobbler

5 dashes of sugar syrup
1 or 2 dashes of brandy
¾ gill of port

Mix well, and strain into a
tumbler half-full of broken

ice. Decorate with fruit, and
serve with a straw.

11th Blue Cooler

The juice of half of a lime
½ gill of white rum
¼ gill of blue curaçao
1 gill of pineapple juice

Stir ingredients in a tumbler.
Add ice. Serve with straws.

A delicious drink – and
what a colour!

12th Bermudian Rose Cocktail

⅓ gill of dry gin
⅙ gill of apricot brandy
⅙ gill of grenadine
⅙ gill of lemon juice

Use the shaker. Decorate
with a slice of fresh apricot,
if available, and a cherry.

13th Brandy Flip

The yolk of one egg
½ gill of brandy
Sugar or sugar syrup to taste

Prepare in the shaker, half
filled with broken ice. Shake
well, and strain into a wine-

glass: serve with grated
nutmeg on top.

14th Millionaire Cocktail (2)

1 dash of grenadine
The juice of one lime
⅙ gill of apricot brandy

⅙ gill of rum
⅙ gill of sloe gin

Use the shaker. Decorate
with a cherry.

15th Sloe Gin Rickey

The juice of half a lime
¾ gill of sloe gin

Mix in a tumbler with a
lump of ice. Fill up with

soda water, stir well, and
serve with a slice of lime.

 From left: Brandy Flip, Sloe Gin Rickey, King Cole Cocktail, Millionaire Cocktail, Port Cobbler, Blue Cooler, Bermudian Rose Cocktail.

SEPTEMBER

DRAMBUIE

16th Rusty Nail Cocktail

⅙ gill of Drambuie
⅓ gill of Scotch whisky

Serve in old-fashioned glass
on ice.

Drambuie is the oldest
of the whisky liqueurs,
the main ingredients
being heather, honey
and whisky.

17th Stars and Stripes – a Pousse Café

Equal parts of:
Crème de cassis
Maraschino
Green Chartreuse

Serve in a pousse café glass,
adding ingredients in the
stated order to form a
layered effect. Pour liqueurs

over the back of a spoon,
held so that it touches the
sides of the glass.

A steady hand is a necessary
ingredient here.

18th Jersey Lily – a Pousse Café

Equal parts of:
Yellow Chartreuse
Old brandy

Serve as above.

Any brandy will float in
just the same way.

19th After Dinner Cocktail (1)

The juice and grated rind of one
lime
¼ gill of apricot brandy
¼ gill of Cointreau

Use the shaker. Serve with a
slice of orange.

20th Hot Scotch

The juice of one lemon
2 lumps of sugar
½ gill of Scotch whisky

Put ingredients in a glass, fill
up with boiling water, stir
well.

21st After Supper Cocktail

4 dashes of fresh lemon juice
¼ gill of Cointreau
¼ gill of apricot brandy

Use the shaker.

22nd Bobby Burns Cocktail

3 dashes of Bénédictine
¼ gill of Italian vermouth
¼ gill of Scotch whisky

Use the mixing glass. Serve
with a little lemon-peel juice
squeezed on top and a
cherry.

84

Clockwise from top left: After Supper Cocktail, Bobby Burns Cocktail, After Dinner Cocktail, Stars and Stripes, Jersey Lily, Hot Scotch, Rusty Nail Cocktail.

SEPTEMBER

IRISH WHISKEY

23rd Irish Coffee

Hot coffee
2 teaspoonsful of sugar
⅓ gill of Irish whiskey
Fresh double cream

Pour coffee into a glass, stir in sugar and whiskey. Pour cream over the back of a warmed spoon, very gently. Do not stir.

24th Paddy Cocktail

1 dash of Angostura bitters
¼ gill of Italian vermouth
¼ gill of Irish whiskey

Use the mixing glass.

25th Southern Gin Cocktail

2 dashes of orange bitters
2 dashes of Cointreau
½ gill of dry gin

Use the shaker. Serve with a little lemon-peel juice squeezed on top.

26th Shamrock Cocktail

3 dashes of green Chartreuse
3 dashes of green crème de menthe
¼ gill of French vermouth
¼ gill of Irish whiskey

Use the mixing glass.

27th Drambuie Swizzle

½ gill of Drambuie
¼ gill of lime cordial
1 drop of orange bitters
Soda water

Half fill a tumbler with ice, add Drambuie, lime cordial and bitters. Top up with soda water, stir. Decorate with a sprig of mint, or a slice of lime.

28th Johnnie Mack Cocktail

3 dashes of pernod
⅙ gill of orange curaçao
⅓ gill of sloe gin

Use the mixing glass. Serve with a little lemon-peel juice squeezed on top.

29th Prairie Oyster Cocktail

The yolk of one egg
2 dashes of vinegar
1 teaspoonful of Worcester sauce
1 teaspoonful of tomato ketchup

Mix all the ingredients except the egg-yolk. Then drop the egg-yolk in the glass without breaking it.

Serve with a dash of pepper on the top.

A real pick-me-up!

 Clockwise from top: Johnnie Mack Cocktail, Paddy Cocktail, Shamrock Cocktail, Drambuie Swizzle, Prairie Oyster, Irish Coffee, Southern Gin Cocktail (centre).

DARK AND GOLDEN RUM

30th Rum Fix

1 teaspoonful of sugar syrup
The juice of half a lemon
1/4 gill dark or white rum
1/4 gill of cherry brandy
A little water to taste

Place ingredients in a tumbler, stir. Fill up glass with crushed ice. Decorate with fruit and serve with straws.

1st Sensation Cocktail

3 dashes of maraschino
3 sprigs of fresh mint
1/8 gill of fresh lemon juice
3/8 gill of dry gin

Use the shaker. Serve with a cherry and fresh mint, if available.

2nd Bitter Cocktail

The juice of a lemon
The juice of half an orange
3 dashes of Angostura bitters

Use the shaker, half-filled with broken ice, and strain into a wine-glass. A little sugar or sugar syrup may be added, according to taste.

You could try this at breakfast time.

3rd Raspberry Cooler

1/4 gill of raspberry syrup
1/4 gill of dry gin
1/8 gill of lime juice

2 dashes of grenadine
1 dash of maraschino
1/3 pint of ginger ale

Place ingredients in a mixing glass. Stir. Pour into a tumbler half-filled with ice.

4th West Indian Cocktail

4 dashes of Angostura bitters
3 dashes of fresh lemon juice
3 dashes of sugar syrup

1 lump of ice
1/2 gill of dry gin

Stir and serve in the same glass.

5th Jamaican Coffee

Hot coffee
2 teaspoonsful of sugar
1/3 gill of dark rum
Fresh double cream

Pour coffee into a glass, stir in sugar and rum. Pour cream over back of a warmed spoon, very gently.

DO NOT STIR.

An after dinner treat.

6th Blue Hawaiian

1/4 gill of white rum
1/8 gill of blue curaçao
1/2 gill of pineapple juice
1/4 gill of coconut cream

Blend with a scoop of crushed ice for a few seconds, and serve in a champagne flute with a cherry and a slice of pineapple.

 Clockwise from left: Sensation Cocktail, Rum Fix, Blue Hawaiian, West Indian Cocktail, Raspberry Cooler, Jamaican Coffee, Bitter Cocktail.

OCTOBER

KALHUA

7th Gin Cobbler

1 teaspoonful of sugar syrup
1 teaspoonful of blue curaçao
1 gill of gin

Shake or mix well, and strain into a tumbler half-full of broken ice. Decorate with fruit and serve with a straw.

8th Whisky Smash

½ lump of sugar
4 sprigs of fresh mint
½ gill of Scotch whisky

In a shaker dissolve the sugar in a little water (or soda water). Add the sprigs of mint, muddle slightly, then remove them. Half-fill the shaker with ice and add whisky. Shake well, the strain into a wine glass, filled with ice. Stir, decorate with a sprig of mint or fruit, and serve with short straws.

9th Milk Punch

½ gill of brandy
¼ gill of dark rum
1 tablespoonful of sugar syrup
Balance of milk

This may be prepared cold (in the shaker, half-filled with broken ice) or hot (by heating the milk). Serve with grated nutmeg on top.

10th Atta Boy Cocktail

4 dashes of grenadine
⅙ gill of French vermouth
⅓ gill of dry gin

Use the shaker. Serve with a little lemon-peel juice squeezed on top.

11th Black Russia Cocktail

⅙ gill of vodka
⅙ gill of kalhua

Stir and serve on ice.

Kalhua originates from Mexico, it is a coffee liqueur.

12th Brave Bull Cocktail

⅙ gill of tequila
⅙ gill of kalhua

Over ice. Use old-fashioned glass.

13th Drambuie Shrub

¼ gill of Drambuie
¾ gill of chilled orange juice
1 scoop of lemon water ice

In a goblet mix the Drambuie and orange juice. Top with water ice. Serve with straws and a small spoon. Decorate with a sprig of mint.

 From left: Milk Punch, Gin Cobbler, Black Russia Cocktail, Drambuie Shrub, Whisky Smash, Brave Bull Cocktail, Atta Boy Cocktail.

OCTOBER

14th Picon Grenadine

½ gill of Amer Picon
⅙ gill of grenadine
(pomegranate)

Mix and serve this aperitif in
the same glass, add water or
soda water and a lump of
ice. Stir and serve.

15th Blenton Cocktail

1 dash of Angostura bitters
⅙ gill of French (or dry
Martini) vermouth
⅓ gill of Plymouth gin

Use the shaker. Serve with a
cherry and a little lemon-
peel juice squeezed and then
served on top.

16th Apricot Lady

¼ gill of golden rum
¼ gill of apricot brandy
⅛ gill of fresh lime juice
3 dashes of orange curaçao
2 dashes of egg white

Blend with a small scoop of
crushed ice for a few
seconds. Serve in a large
wine glass with a slice of
orange.

17th Daiquiri Cocktail

⅓ gill of white rum
⅑ gill of fresh lime or lemon
juice
2 teaspoonsful of sugar

Use the shaker.

18th Apple Pie Cocktail

2 dashes of apricot brandy
¼ gill of bacardi rum
¼ gill of Italian vermouth

Use the shaker.

19th Knickerbocker Cocktail

1 dash of Italian vermouth
⅙ gill of French vermouth
⅓ gill of dry gin

Use the mixing glass. Serve
with a little lemon-peel juice
squeezed on top.

20th Whisky Fix

2 teaspoonsful of sugar syrup
The juice of half a lemon
¾ gill of Scotch whisky
water to taste

Place ingredients in a
tumbler, stir. Fill up glass
with crushed ice. Decorate
with fruit and serve with
straws.

From left: Picon Grenadine, Blenton Cocktail, Daiquiri Cocktail, Apricot Lady, Knickerbocker Cocktail, Apple Pie Cocktail, Whisky Fix.

GRAND MARNIER

21st Adonis Cocktail

1 dash of orange bitters
⅓ gill of dry sherry
⅙ gill of Italian vermouth

Use the mixing glass. Serve with a piece of orange.

22nd Alice Mine Cocktail

2 dashes of Scotch whisky
¼ gill of Italian vermouth
¼ gill of kummel

Use the mixing glass. Serve with a cherry.

23rd Blue Boar

⅜ gill of vodka
⅛ gill of Drambuie
⅛ gill of blue curaçao

1 dash of lemon squash
The white of 1 egg

Use the shaker. Serve with a fresh flower.

24th Artist's Special Cocktail

For four persons:
⅓ gill of fresh lemon juice
⅓ gill of gooseberry syrup

⅔ gill of dry sherry
⅔ gill of Scotch whisky

Use the mixing glass. Serve with a slice of lemon.

25th Yellow Daisy Cocktail

1 dash of pernod
⅕ gill of French vermouth
¹⁄₁₀ gill of Grand Marnier
⅕ gill of dry gin

Use the shaker. Serve with a cherry.

26th Trocadero Cocktail

1 dash of orange bitters
1 dash of grenadine
¼ gill of French vermouth
¼ gill of Italian vermouth

Use the mixing glass. Serve with a cherry and a little

lemon-peel juice squeezed on top.

27th Allies Cocktail

2 dashes of kummel
¼ gill of French vermouth
¼ gill of dry gin

Use the shaker.

 From left: Artist's Special Cocktail, Allies Cocktail, Yellow Daisy Cocktail, Trocadero Cocktail, Blue Boar Cocktail, Alice Mine Cocktail, Adonis Cocktail.

28th Brandy Punch

The juice of half a lemon
1 tablespoonful of sugar syrup
2 or 3 dashes of Cointreau
¾ gill of brandy

Prepare in a shaker, half-filled with broken ice. Strain into an ice-filled tumbler.

Decorate with seasonal fruits.

29th Port Wine Flip

The yolk of one egg
½ gill of port
Sugar syrup to taste

Prepare in a shaker, half-filled with broken ice. Shake well, and strain into a wine

glass. Serve with grated nutmeg on top.

30th Macaroni Cocktail

⅙ gill of Italian vermouth
⅓ gill of pernod

Use the mixing glass.

31st Satan's Whiskers Cocktail

1 dash of orange bitters
⅒ gill of fresh orange juice
⅒ gill of French vermouth

⅒ gill of Italian vermouth
⅒ gill of Grand Marnier
⅒ gill of dry gin

Use the shaker. Serve with a slice of orange.

Hallowe'en.

1st Amaretto Sour

¼ gill of fresh lemon juice
½ gill of Amaretto di Saronno

Make in a shaker, half-filled with broken ice. Strain into a frosted tulip champagne glass. Decorate with a slice of orange.

* To frost the glass: moisten edges with lemon juice then dip in castor sugar.

This delicious Italian liqueur was first made in Saronno in the sixteenth century.

2nd Blushing Barmaid

¼ gill of Amaretto di Saronno
¼ gill of Campari
The white of ½ egg
½ gill of bitter lemon

Shake Amaretto di Saronno, Campari and egg white with broken ice. Strain into an ice-filled glass. Top up with

bitter lemon, stir. Decorate with slices of lemon and fresh apricot and a cherry.

3rd Orange Bloom Cocktail

⅛ gill of Cointreau
⅛ gill of Italian vermouth
¼ gill of dry gin

Use the shaker. Serve with a cherry.

4th Quiet Sunday

½ gill of vodka
¼ gill of Amaretto di Saronno
1 gill of fresh orange juice
1 dash of grenadine

Mix vodka, Amaretto di Saronno and orange juice in a shaker, half-filled with ice.

Strain into an ice-filled tumbler, then add a dash of grenadine.

A super drink any day of the week.

Mischief Night! – autumn's equivalent to April Fool Day.

 Clockwise from top: Amaretto Sour, Quiet Sunday Cocktail, Orange Bloom Cocktail, Brandy Punch, Macaroni Cocktail, Blushing Barmaid Cocktail, Port Wine Flip, Satan's Whiskers Cocktail (centre).

NOVEMBER

5th Oxford Punch

3 parts of dark rum
2 parts of brandy
1 part of lemon squash
6 parts of boiling water
Sugar to taste

This is a modern version of a traditional recipe. It can be used for any number of persons, provided that the proportions of the ingredients are kept the same.

Guy Fawkes Night. A warming drink after the bonfire has died down.

6th Blackcurrant Tea (non-alcoholic)

1 tablespoonful of blackcurrant jelly
1 dessertspoonful of lemon juice
4 lumps of sugar

Mix together in a jug, and add a tumblerful of boiling water. Stir well, and stand the jug in a pan of boiling water for twenty minutes. Then strain and serve.

Perfect for the children – or those with a sweet tooth.

7th Drambuie Coffee

Hot coffee
2 teaspoonsful of sugar
1/3 gill of Drambuie
Fresh double cream

Pour coffee into a glass, stir in sugar and Drambuie. Pour cream over the back of a warmed spoon, very gently. DO NOT STIR.

8th Gluhwein

2 gills of red wine
1 slice of lemon
1 slice of orange

2 lumps of sugar
pinch of cinnamon

Heat all ingredients.

A lovely warming drink, a favourite in ski resorts.

9th Hot Tea Punch

3 pints of freshly brewed tea
1 pint of brandy
1 bottle of dark rum
Sugar to taste

Mix well, and mull with a red-hot poker. Decorate with orange and lemon peel. This should be enough for at least twelve persons.

10th Port Wine Egg Nog

1 egg
1 teaspoonful of sugar syrup
3/4 gill of port

1/4 gill of brandy
1/4 gill of rum
1 gill milk

Prepare in a shaker, half-filled with broken ice. Strain into a glass, sprinkle with grated nutmeg. Stir in more milk if desired.

11th Scotch Milk Punch

3/4 gill of Scotch whisky
3 dashes of lemon juice
1 tablespoonful of sugar syrup
Balance of milk

This may be prepared cold (in a shaker, half-filled with broken ice) or hot (by heating the milk). Serve with grated nutmeg on top.

Clockwise from left: Hot Tea Punch, Port Wine Egg Nog, Scotch Milk Punch, Drambuie Coffee, Gluhwein, Blackcurrant Tea, Oxford Punch.

WHITE CRÈME DE MENTHE

12th Stinger Cocktail

⅛ gill of white crème de menthe
⅜ gill of brandy

Use the shaker. Serve very cold.

Try this cocktail after dinner as crème de menthe has very good digestive properties.

13th Lord Suffolk Cocktail

For four persons:
¼ gill of maraschino
¼ gill of Cointreau

¼ gill of Italian vermouth
1¼ gills of dry gin

Use the shaker. Serve with a little lemon-peel juice squeezed on top.

14th Brandy Collins

1 teaspoonful of sugar syrup
The juice of one lemon or 2 limes
¾ gill of brandy

Make in a shaker, half-filled with broken ice. Strain into a tumbler, add ice and fill

up with soda water. Stir. Decorate with fruit. Serve with straws.

15th Pall Mall Cocktail

1 dash of orange bitters
1 teaspoonful of white crème de menthe

⅙ gill of French vermouth
⅙ gill of Italian vermouth
⅙ gill of dry gin

Use the mixing glass.

This liqueur has exactly the same flavour as the better known green crème de menthe. No colour has been added.

16th Brandy Highball

¾ gill of brandy
Ginger ale or soda water

Serve in a tumbler with a few lumps of ice. Serve with

a piece of lemon peel or a slice of lemon.

17th Golden Cadillac Cocktail

⅙ gill of Galliano
⅙ gill of white curaçao or
Cointreau
⅙ gill of cream

Use the shaker.

18th Martini Cocktail (medium)

⅛ gill of French (or dry Martini) vermouth
⅛ gill of Italian vermouth
¼ gill of dry gin

Use the mixing glass. Serve with a little lemon-peel juice squeezed and then served on top.

Clockwise from top left: Golden Cadillac Cocktail, Brandy Collins, Brandy Highball, Stinger Cocktail, Martini Cocktail, Lord Suffolk Cocktail, Pall Mall Cocktail.

LILLET

19th Napoleon Cocktail

1 dash of orange curaçao
1 dash of Fernet Branca
1 dash of Dubonnet
½ gill of dry gin

Use the mixing glass. Serve with a cherry and a little lemon-peel juice squeezed on top.

20th Whisky Collins

1 teaspoonful of sugar syrup
The juice of one lemon or 2 limes
¾ gill of Scotch whisky

Use the shaker, half-filled with broken ice. Strain into a tumbler, add ice and fill

up with soda water. Stir. Decorate with fruit. Serve with straws.

21st Emmagreen

¼ gill of dry gin
⅛ gill of fresh orange juice
⅛ gill of Amaretto di Saronno
⅛ gill of blue curaçao
white of ½ egg

generous ½ gill well-chilled sparkling wine or champagne

Half-fill a shaker with broken ice. Add gin, orange juice, Amaretto di Saronno, blue curaçao and egg white.

Shake, strain into a frosted tumbler and top up with champagne.
* To frost the glass: moisten the rim of the glass with blue curaçao, then dip in castor sugar.

A really colourful experience!

22nd 'Hoop La!' Cocktail

⅛ gill of fresh lemon juice
⅛ gill of Lillet
⅛ gill of Cointreau
⅛ gill of brandy

Use the shaker. Serve with a slice of orange.

Lillet is a vermouth-type drink.

23rd Dubonnet Citron

½ gill of Dubonnet
⅙ gill of sirop de citron (lemon)

Mix and serve this apéritif in the same glass. Add water or soda water and a lump of ice. Stir and serve.

* As alternatives to Dubonnet use Amer Picon, Lillet or Campari.

24th Bamboo or Reform Cocktail

1 dash of orange bitters
¼ gill of dry sherry
¼ gill of French vermouth

Use the mixing glass. Serve with a little lemon-peel juice squeezed on top.

25th 'Hoots Mon' Cocktail

⅛ gill of Lillet
⅛ gill of Italian vermouth
¼ gill of Scotch whisky

Use the mixing glass.

Clockwise from top left: Napoleon Cocktail, Whisky Collins, Emmagreen, Hoop-la Cocktail, Bamboo Cocktail, Hoots-Mon Cocktail, Dubonnet Citron.

CRÈME DE CACAO

26th Winter Sunrise

¼ gill of Campari
¼ gill of dry gin
1 gill of pineapple juice

Pour into a tumbler, fill up with ice, stir. Decorate with fruit.

27th Rum Collins

1 teaspoonful of sugar syrup
The juice of one lemon or two limes
¾ gill of rum (white or dark)

Make in a shaker, half-filled with broken ice. Strain into a tumbler, add ice and fill up with soda water. Stir.

Decorate with fruit. Serve with straws.

28th Alaska Cocktail

2 dashes of orange bitters
⅛ gill of yellow Chartreuse
⅜ gill of dry gin

Use the shaker. Serve with a little lemon-peel juice squeezed on top.

29th Alexander Cocktail (1)

⅙ gill of crème de cacao
⅙ gill of sweetened cream
⅙ gill of brandy

Use the shaker. Decorate with some grated chocolate.

Crème de cacao is a sweet cocoa/vanilla flavoured liqueur. It comes from Cacao, a part of Venezuela.

30th Old-Fashioned Cocktail

1 lump of sugar
2 dashes of Angostura bitters
¾ gill of Canadian Club whisky
Peel of half a lemon

Prepare and serve in a tumbler. Put the sugar in first, then add the Angostura bitters, and muddle. Add the whisky and a cube of ice, and stir. Squeeze lemon-peel juice on top, and serve with a piece of lemon-peel in the glass.

St Andrew's Day. (Patron Saint of Scotland.)

1st Alexander Cocktail (2)

⅛ gill of crème de cacao
⅛ gill of sweetened cream
¼ gill of dry gin

Use the shaker. Decorate with a chocolate flake.

Try the Alexander cocktails after dinner.

2nd Martinez Cocktail

1 dash of orange bitters
2 dashes of maraschino
¼ gill of French vermouth
¼ gill of dry gin

Use the mixing glass. Serve with an olive and a little lemon-peel juice squeezed on top.

 From left: Alexander Cocktail (2), Martinez Cocktail, Rum Collins, Old-Fashioned Cocktail, Winter Sunrise, Alexander Cocktail (1), Alaska Cocktail.

DECEMBER

TIA MARIA

3rd Spanish Town Cocktail

2 or 3 dashes of Cointreau
½ gill of white rum

Use the shaker.

4th Blue Crusta

⅓ gill of blue curaçao
⅙ gill of lemon juice
1 dash of Angostura bitters
1 teaspoonful of brandy

Make in a shaker half-filled with broken ice. Place a spiral of lemon rind in a frosted crusta (small wine) glass. Add ice and strained

cocktail. Decorate with fruit. * To frost the glass: moisten edges with curaçao then dip in castor sugar.

5th Special Pousse Café

1 teaspoonful of grenadine
⅙ gill of green crème de menthe
1 teaspoonful of Galliano
⅙ gill of kummel
⅙ gill of brandy

Serve in a pousse café glass, add ingredients in stated order to form a layered effect. Pour liquids over the

back of a spoon held so that it touches the sides of the glass.

6th Calypso Coffee

Hot coffee
2 teaspoonsful of sugar
⅙ gill of Tia Maria
⅙ gill of light rum
Fresh double cream

Pour coffee into a wine glass, stir in sugar, Tia Maria and light rum. Pour cream over

the back of a warmed spoon, very gently. DO NOT STIR.

7th Angel's Tip Cocktail

⅓ gill of crème de cacao
⅑ gill of fresh cream

Float cream on top. Decorate with a little grated chocolate.

8th Grasshopper Cocktail

⅙ gill of green crème de menthe
⅙ gill of white crème de cacao
⅙ gill of fresh cream

Shake and serve in champagne glass with straws.

9th Newton's Special Cocktail

1 dash of Angostura bitters
⅛ gill of Cointreau
⅜ gill of brandy

Use the mixing glass.

 From left: Blue Crusta, Angel's Tip Cocktail, Grasshopper Cocktail, Newton's Special Cocktail, Special Pousse Café, Calypso Coffee, Spanish Town Cocktail.

DECEMBER

KIRSCH

10th Crow Cocktail

1 dash of grenadine
⅓ gill of fresh lemon juice
⅙ gill of Scotch whisky

Use the mixing glass.

11th Rum Highball

¾ gill of white or dark rum
Lemonade or soda water

Serve in a tumbler with a few lumps of ice. Serve with a piece of lime peel or a slice of lime.

12th Mary Pickford Cocktail

3 dashes of grenadine
6 drops of maraschino
¼ gill of fresh pineapple juice
¼ gill of bacardi rum

Use the mixing glass.

13th Raffles Knockout Cocktail

⅓ gill of Kirsch
⅓ gill of Cointreau
1 dash of fresh lemon

Shake, and serve in champagne glass. Add cherries.

Kirsch is a colourless brandy made from wild cherries and their stones.

14th Hot Fruit Drinks

Fruit syrup
The juice of one lemon
Sugar to taste

Dilute one part of fruit syrup with two parts of hot water, add the sugar and lemon juice, and serve.

15th K.C.B. Cocktail

1 dash of apricot brandy
1 dash of fresh lemon juice
⅛ gill of kirsch
⅜ gill of dry gin

Use the shaker. Serve with a little lemon-peel juice squeezed on top.

16th Gin Highball

¾ gill of dry gin
2 dashes of Angostura bitters
Soda water

Serve in a tumbler with a few lumps of ice, a piece of lemon peel or a slice of lemon.

From left: Crow Cocktail, K.C.B. Cocktail, Gin Highball, Rum Highball,
Raffles Knockout Cocktail, Mary Pickford Cocktail, Hot Fruit Drink.

DECEMBER

17th Port Wine Negus

1 wine-glassful of port wine
1 lemon
Sugar to taste

Put the wine in a long glass, and add the sugar and the rind and juice of the lemon.

Fill up with boiling water, and strain.

A great drink for unexpected guests – perhaps the carol singers!

18th Three Miller Cocktail

3 dashes of grenadine
1 dash of fresh lemon juice
⅙ gill of bacardi rum
⅓ gill of brandy

Use the shaker.

19th Heart Stirrer

¼ gill of Amaretto di Saronno
Chilled Veuve di Vernay or dry sparkling white wine

Pour Amaretto di Saronno into a champagne glass, top

up with wine, stir carefully.

A very special drink.

20th Vermouth Cassis Highball

¾ gill of French vermouth
1 teaspoonful crème de cassis
Soda water or lemonade

Serve in a tumbler with a few lumps of ice, and cherry,

and a piece of lemon peel or a slice of lemon.

21st Buck's Fizz Cocktail

Juice of an orange
Top with champagne

Use large goblet or champagne glass.

A classic cocktail – a lovely party drink.

22nd Orient Express

⅙ gill of Drambuie
⅙ gill of Canadian Club whisky
⅙ gill of French vermouth

Use the mixing glass. Stir ingredients in equal proportions over ice. Strain

into cocktail glass. Serve with a piece of orange peel.

23rd After Dinner Blues

¼ gill of blue curaçao
⅛ gill of fresh double cream

Float the cream on the curaçao. DO NOT STIR.

Clockwise from top left: Port Wine Negus, Heart Stirrer, Buck's Fizz Cocktail, Vermouth Cassis Highball, After Dinner Blues, Orient Express Cocktail, Three Miller Cocktail.

DECEMBER

24th Grand Slam Cocktail

⅛ gill of French vermouth
⅛ gill of Italian vermouth
¼ gill of Swedish punch

Use the mixing glass. Serve
with a slice of lemon.

Try leaving this one for
Santa, after you've
made it for your guests!

25th Monte Carlo Imperial Cocktail

⅛ gill of fresh lemon juice
⅛ gill of green crème de menthe
¼ gill of dry gin

Use the shaker. Strain into a
wine-glass, and fill up with
champagne.

A festive drink for
Christmas Day.

26th Whisky Sangaree

1 teaspoonful of sugar
½ gill of water
¾ gill of Scotch whisky

Dissolve sugar in the water
in a whisky tumbler. Add
whisky and fill with crushed
ice. Stir well, decorate with
grated nutmeg. Serve with
straws.

27th Normandy Coffee

Hot coffee
2 teaspoonsful of sugar
⅓ gill of Bénédictine
Fresh double cream

Pour coffee into a glass, stir
in sugar and Bénédictine.
Pour cream over the back of
a warmed spoon, very
gently. DO NOT STIR.

28th Hot Buttered Rum

2 tablespoonfuls of dark rum
2 teaspoonfuls of sugar
2 teaspoonfuls of butter

½ teaspoonful of mixed spices
(cinnamon and cloves)

Put the ingredients in a
tumbler, fill up with boiling
water, and stir well.

29th Grenadier Cocktail

3 dashes of grenadine
¼ gill of ginger wine
¼ gill of brandy

Use the shaker. Serve with a
strawberry or a slice of
orange.

30th Prairie Hen Cocktail

2 dashes of vinegar
1 teaspoonful of Worcester sauce
1 egg

2 dashes of tabasco sauce
Pepper and salt

Mix all the ingredients
except the egg. Then drop
the egg in the glass without
breaking it.

A real Pick-me-up
between Christmas and
New Year festivities.

31st Zombie

¼ gill of white rum
¼ gill of dark rum
¼ gill of apricot brandy
⅛ gill of orange juice

⅛ gill of lemon juice
⅛ gill of pineapple juice
A little 151% proof Demararan
rum

Use the shaker for all the
ingredients except the

Demararan rum. Strain and
pour into a highball glass
half-filled with crushed ice.
Pour over the Demararan
rum. Garnish with slices of
pineapple, orange, lemon
and lime.

A fitting end to the
year. This is the most
lethal cocktail of them
all.

 Clockwise from bottom left: Hot Buttered Rum, Prairie Hen, Grand Slam Cocktail, Monte Carlo Imperial Cocktail, Grenadier Cocktail, Normandy Coffee, Whisky Sangaree, Zombie Cocktail (centre).

Ingredients Guide

If you have just one or two bottles in your drinks cabinet, this guide will help you to find the cocktails you can make using them. Since most cocktails are based on gin, brandy, rum, vermouth, Scotch whisky, Canadian Club whisky or vodka the cocktails are listed under those headings. To find, for example, a cocktail containing Gin and White Rum, look under the main heading Gin-based Cocktails and then under the sub-heading Gin/White Rum. The two cocktails you will find listed here do not also appear under Rum-based cocktails, avoiding repetition. Mixers and non-alcoholic extras (see page 8 for the list of these) are not included in the ingredients guide.

Gin-based Cocktails

Gin only
Belmont Cocktail
Bennett Cocktail
Bulldog Cooler
Café de Paris Cocktail
Clover Club Cocktail
Cream Fizz
Gimlet Cocktail
Gin Daisy
Gin Fix
Gin Highball
Gin Sling
Grape Vine Cocktail
Hot Gin
Orange Blossom Cocktail (1)
Orange Blossom Cocktail (2)
Orange Fizz
Pink Lady Cocktail
Pink Rose Cocktail
Raspberry Cooler
Royal Fizz
Silver Fizz
Strawberry Cream Cooler
Strawberry Dawn
West Indian Cocktail
White Cocktail
Whiz-bang Cooler

Gin/rum
Bacardi Special Cocktail
Roosevelt Cocktail

Gin/vermouth
Atta Boy Cocktail
Bloodhound Cocktail
Cooperstown Cocktail
Knickerbocker Cocktail
Martini Cocktail (dry)
Martini Cocktail (medium)

Martini Cocktail (sweet)
Polo Cocktail
Queen's Cocktail
R.A.C. Cocktail
Velocity Cocktail
Yellow Rattler Cocktail

Gin/vermouth/apricot brandy
Western Rose Cocktail

Gin/vermouth/calvados
Star Cocktail

Gin/vermouth/Campari
Cardinale Cocktail
Negroni Cocktail

Gin/vermouth/Cointreau
Journalist Cocktail
Luigi Cocktail
Orange Bloom Cocktail

Gin/vermouth/crème de cassis
Parisian Cocktail

Gin/vermouth/Dubonnet
Café Royal Appetiser Cocktail
Dubonnet Cocktail
Royal Cocktail

Gin/vermouth/Grand Marnier
Satan's Whiskers Cocktail

Gin/vermouth/green Chartreuse
Sandmartin Cocktail

Gin/vermouth/kummel
Allies Cocktail

Gin/vermouth/maraschino
Martinez Cocktail

Gin/vermouth/sherry
Inca Cocktail

Gin/apricot brandy
Bermudian Rose Cocktail
Fairy Belle Cocktail
Paradise Cocktail

Gin/apricot brandy/calvados
Angel Face Cocktail
Prince's Smile Cocktail

Gin/blue curaçao
Blue Bird Cocktail
Gin Cobbler

Gin/Campari
Tropical Dawn
Winter Sunrise

Gin/cherry brandy
Singapore Sling

Gin/Cherry Brandy/Bénédictine
Straits Sling

Gin/Cointreau
Hula-hula Cocktail
Hawaiian Cocktail
Pegu Club Cocktail
Southern Gin Cocktail

Gin/crème de cassis
Cassis Highball

Gin/crème de menthe
Alexander's Sister Cocktail
Fallen Angel Cocktail
Monte Carlo Imperial Cocktail

Gin/crème de menthe/kummel
Green Dragon Cocktail

Gin/kummel
Silver Streak Cocktail

Gin/maraschino
Gin Crusta
Sensation Cocktail
White Rose Cocktail

Gin/pernod
Café de Paris Cocktail
London Cocktail
Monkey Gland Cocktail

Gin/pernod/calvados
Dempsey Cocktail

Gin/sherry
Roc-a-coe Cocktail

Gin/Swedish punch
Waldorf Cocktail

Brandy-based Cocktails

Brandy only
Brandy Collins
Brandy Daisy
Brandy Flip
Brandy Highball
Brandy Julep
Brandy Smash
Brandy Sour
Cider Cup (1)
Grenadier Cocktail
Plain Egg Nog

Brandy/white rum
Hot Tea Punch
Oxford Punch
Scorpion
Three Miller Cocktail

Brandy/white rum/port
Port Wine Egg Nog

Brandy/vermouth
Charles Cocktail

Washington Cocktail

Brandy/vermouth/Bénédictine
Fioupe Cocktail

Brandy/vermouth/pernod
Presto Cocktail

Brandy/apricot brandy
Cuban Cocktail

Brandy/blue curaçao
Blue Crusta
Bosom Caresser Cocktail
Breakfast Egg Nog
East India Cocktail

Brandy/calvados
Depth Bomb Cocktail
Depth Charge Cocktail

Brandy/cherry brandy
Brandy Fix
Vanderbilt Cocktail

Brandy/cherry brandy/orange curaçao
Cherry Blossom Cocktail

Brandy/Cointreau
Brandy Punch
Claret Cup
Egg Sour
Newton's Special Cocktail
Rolls-Royce Cocktail
Sidecar Cocktail

Brandy/crème de menthe
Emerald Cooler

Brandy/green Chartreuse
Champs Elysées Cocktail

Brandy/maraschino
Brandy Crusta

Brandy/orange curaçao
Brandy Cobbler

Brandy/port
Port Cobbler
Port Wine Cocktail

Brandy/yellow Chartreuse
Golden Slipper
Jersey Lily

Brandy/yellow Chartreuse/pernod
Yellow Parrot Cocktail

White Rum-based Cocktails

White rum only
Bacardi Cocktail
Casablanca
Cuba Libre
Daiquiri Cocktail
Piña Colada
Plain Egg Nog
Planter's Cocktail
Rum Collins
Rum Cooler
Rum Highball

Rum/vermouth/apricot brandy
Apple Pie Cocktail

Rum/vermouth/blue curaçao
Fair and Warmer Cocktail

Rum/apricot brandy/sloe gin
Millionaire Cocktail (2)

Rum/blue curaçao
Blue Cooler
Blue Hawaiian

Rum/brown or orange curaçao
Rum Daisy

Rum/cherry brandy
Rum Fix

Rum/Cointreau
Spanish Town Cocktail
Spring Shake-up

Rum/crème de banane
Banana Bliss
Banana Daiquiri

Rum/Galliano
Barracuda

Rum/maraschino
Mary Pickford Cocktail
Rum Crusta

Rum/pernod
Bacardi Crusta

Rum/sherry
Quarterdeck Cocktail

Rum/Swedish punch
Melba Cocktail
Tanglefoot Cocktail

Rum/Swedish punch calvados
Roulette Cocktail
Twelve Miles Out Cocktail

Vermouth-based Cocktails

Vermouth only
Addington Cocktail
Club Cooler
Raymond Hitch Cocktail
Trocadero Cocktail
Wyoming Swing Cocktail

Vermouth/Scotch whisky
Affinity Cocktail
Oppenheim Cocktail
Rob Roy Cocktail
Thistle Cocktail
Wembley Cocktail

Vermouth/Scotch whisky/Bénédictine
Bobby Burns Cocktail

*Vermouth/Scotch whisky/
cherry Brandy*
Blood and Sand Cocktail

Vermouth/Scotch whisky/kummel
Alice Mine Cocktail

Vermouth/Canadian Club whisky
Hot Deck Cocktail
Los Angeles Cocktail
Manhattan Cocktail (dry)
Mountain Cocktail

*Vermouth/Canadian club whisky/
Amer Picon*
Creole Cocktail

*Vermouth/Canadian Club
whisky/Campari*
Old Pal Cocktail

*Vermouth/Canadian Club
whisky/Cointreau*
Oriental Cocktail

*Vermouth/Canadian Club
whisky/Drambuie*
Orient Express

*Vermouth/Canadian Club
whisky/Dubonnet*
Soul's Kiss Cocktail

*Vermouth/Canadian Club
whisky/Swedish Punch*

Boomerang Cocktail

Vermouth/vodka
Vodkatini Cocktail

Vermouth/Amer Picon
Picon Cocktail

Vermouth/crème de cassis
Crème de Cassis Highball

*Vermouth/green Chartreuse/
Plymouth gin*
Bijou Cocktail

Vermouth/Irish whiskey
Paddy Cocktail

*Vermouth/Irish whiskey/
crème de menthe*
Shamrock Cocktail

Vermouth/maraschino
Diplomat Cocktail

Vermouth/sherry
Bamboo or Reform Cocktail
Greenbriar Cocktail

Vermouth/sloe gin
Blackthorn Cocktail
Sloe Gin Cocktail

Vermouth/Swedish punch
Grand Slam Cocktail

Scotch whisky-based Cocktails

Scotch whisky only
Crow Cocktail
Gaelic Coffee
Hot Scotch
Scotch Milk Punch
Scotch Mist Cocktail
Whisky Collins
Whisky Cooler
Whisky Daisy
Whisky Fix
Whisky Rickey
Whisky Sangaree
Whisky Smash
Whisky Sour
Whisky Toddy

Scotch whisky/Bénédictine
'Oh, Henry!' Cocktail

Scotch whisky/Fernet Branca
King Cole Cocktail

Scotch whisky/pernod
Linstead Cocktail
Morning Glory Fizz
White Horse Daisy

Scotch whisky/sherry
Artist's Special Cocktail

Canadian Club whisky-based
Cocktails

Canadian Club whisky only
Club Cocktail
Commodore Cocktail
Ink Street Cocktail
New York Cocktail
New York Cooler
Old-Fashioned Cocktail
Rock and Rye Cocktail
'S.G.' Cocktail

Canadian Club whisky/blue curaçao
Millionaire Cocktail (1)

*Canadian Club whisky/brown or
orange curaçao*
Rye Fizz

*Canadian Club whisky/
Cointreau/Dubonnet*
Dandy Cocktail

Canadian Club whisky/pernod
Ladies' Cocktail

Vodka-based Cocktails

Vodka only
Bloody Mary
Harvey Wallbanger Cocktail
Salty Dog
Screwdriver Cocktail

Vodka/blue curaçao/Drambuie
Blue Boar

Vodka/Campari
S.W.1. Cocktail

Vodka/Cointreau
Balalaika Cocktail

Vodka/kalhua
Black Russia Cocktail

Types of Cocktail

Party Cocktails
Brandy Punch
Buck's Fizz Cocktail
Champagne Cobbler
Champagne Julep
Cider Cup (1 and 2)
Claret Cup
Gluhwein
Hock Cup
Hot Tea Punch
Moselle Cobbler
Valentine's Champagne Cocktail

Long and Cool Drinks
Angostura Fizz
Applejack Highball
Apricot Lady
Banana Bliss
Banana Daiquiri
Blue Cooler
Brandy Cobbler
Brandy Collins
Brandy Daisy
Brandy Fix
Brandy Highball
Brandy Julep
Brandy Smash
Bulldog Cooler
Casablanca
Cassis Highball
Club Cooler
Cream Fizz
Cuba Libre Cocktail
Drambuie Swizzle
Emerald Cooler
Gin Cobbler
Gin Daisy
Gin Highball
Gin Sling
Ginger Ale Cup
Grape Cocktail
Morning Glory Fizz
New York Cooler
Orange Fizz
Piña Colada
Port Cobbler
Port Wine Sangaree
Raspberry Cooler
Royal Fizz
Rum Collins
Rum Cooler
Rum Daisy
Rum Fix
Rum Highball

Rye Fix
Scorpion
Shandy Gaff
Sherry Sangaree
Silver Fizz
Singapore Sling
Sloe Gin Rickey
Spring Shake-Up
Straits Sling
Strawberry Cream Cooler
Strawberry Dawn
Sundew Cocktail
Sunset Cooler
True Blue
Vermouth Cassis Highball
Whisky Collins
Whisky Cooler
Whisky Daisy
Whisky Rickey
Whisky Sangaree
Whisky Smash
White Horse Daisy
Whiz-Bang Cooler
Wyoming Swing

Non-alcoholic cocktails
Blackcurrant Cocktail
Blackcurrant Tea
Bitter Cocktail
Cherry Cocktail
Egg Lemonade
Egg Punch
Ginger Ale Cup
Grapefruit Drink
Grapefruit and Orangeade
Hot Fruit Drinks
Iced Chocolate
Iced Coffee
Iced Tea
Mixed Fruit Cocktail
Pineapple Lemonade
Pussy Foot Cocktail
Orangeade
Raspberry Lemonade
Sundew Cocktail

Breakfast Cocktails
Bitter Cocktail
Breakfast Egg Nog

Special Occasion Cocktails
Alfonso Cocktail
Barracuda Cocktail
Black Velvet Cocktail
Blue Hawaiian
Buck's Fizz Cocktail
Champagne Cobbler
Champagne Julep

Emmagreen
Golden Dream Cocktail
Heart Stirrer
Kir Royale
Monte Carlo Imperial Cocktail
Valentine's Champagne Cocktail

Coffees
Calypso Coffee
Drambuie Coffee
Gaelic Coffee
Iced Coffee
Irish Coffee
Jamaican Coffee
Normandy Coffee

After Dinner Cocktails
After Dinner Blues
After Dinner Cocktail
After Supper Cocktail
Alexander Cocktail (1 and 2)
Alexander's Sister Cocktail
Angel's Tip Cocktail
Bobby Burns Cocktail
Chocolate Cocktail (1 and 2)
Golden Slipper
Grasshopper Cocktail
Grenadier Cocktail
Jersey Lily
Newton's Special Cocktail
Port Wine Cocktail
Raffles Knockout Cocktail
Rusty Nail Cocktail
Spanish Town Cocktail
Special Pousse Café
Stars and Stripes

Dessert Cocktails
Grapefruit Cocktail (1 and 2)
Drambuie Shrub

Night Caps
Ale Posset
Hot Buttered Rum
Hot Gin
Hot Scotch
Milk Punch
Plain Egg Nog
Port Wine Egg Nog
Port Wine Flip
Port Wine Negus
Scotch Milk Punch
Whisky Toddy

Pick-me-ups
Prairie Hen Cocktail
Prairie Oyster Cocktail

Index (in alphabetical order)